# AND SO I PRAYED...

## The First 40 Days: Special Edition

## LYDIA ELLE

ISBN: 1514398095
ISBN 13: 9781514398098

<u>Praise for 'And So I Prayed...'</u>

" 'And So I Prayed' is a gem. This memoir reads like an effervescent narrative that feeds you on a visceral level. Even as a 40 Day Devotional, I found myself unable to put it down. Lydia is incredibly relatable and approaches the idea and act of prayer in a down to earth - sometimes witty even - way."
- *Candiace Dillard, Miss United States 2013*

"Lydia Elle has written an engaging devotional that invites the reader to share in the ebbs and flows of her spiritual journey. I am genuinely thankful for her transparency throughout the text and the seemingly effortless way she interweaves Biblical trusts and wise counsel throughout her personal experiences. Lydia gives voice to the innermost thoughts of many of her peers, who are often too afraid to express their fears, doubts, and concerns, even to God Himself. Her courageous text is both encouraging and convicting. This compact devotional will be one that readers return to time and time again as the richness of her project provides more than effort material well beyond the initial 40 days.
- Jo Van McCalester, PhD

"Where do I begin?! I finished reading the book weeks ago but was so moved that I couldn't write. I am simply grateful for Lydia's willingness to share this journey. We, as humans get caught up on wanting to know the intricate details of someone's testimony. What I appreciated the most was that instead of all the nitty gritty's, Lydia allowed us to see and experience the details of an awesome God, which is THE sweetest part of the testimony. This is the book and type of book that we need during our worst. Resources that buoy us in the storm, lead us directly to THE greatest source of help and show us how AWEsome and sovereign God is. I was moved, touched, assured and encouraged."
- *Keenda Cadogan*

"This book has been a great accompaniment to my daily devotion. Lydia's transparency sheds light on the path she's traveled. I have been able to identify

with her testimony as I continue my journey on a similar path. Thank you for your testimony and your ministry!"
- Mark Francis


"Often times, authors tell their story, but Lydia tells mine. Her transparency and humility translates to a compelling tale, that speaks of a raw, uninhibited journey to revelation and enlightenment, that culminates into a renewal of hope and strength."
- Charlee Covington

Learn more about me at

www.LydiaElle.com

Connect with me and share what you learned from my journey to help your own. Use the tag below to share your reaction and lessons you learned for my story :

#AndSoIPrayed

Facebook, Twitter, and Instagram - *@iamLydiaElle*
YouTube - *I am Lydia Elle*

*For purchases of 20 or more books :*
Lydia@LydiaElle.com

*To secure a date for the #keepGROWING book tour in your city contact:*
booking@LydiaElle.com

**Special Video Message - Why I wrote 'And So I Prayed...'**

Hear why I wrote the book in an intimate interview:

www.LydiaElle.com/booklinks

Dedicated to my mother, Genifer, who made me - thank you for loving me -
...and my daughter, London, who saved me - because of you, I am.

This book is also dedicated to every soul that had to or is going through a
storm. I promise you that the end will come and you will be so much better
because of this moment.

These are the first 40 days of the rest of your life...

# CONTENTS

Introduction                                    xv

Day 1 - The First 40                             1

Day 2 - Feelings                                 4

Day 3 - I Will Never Know                        7

Day 4 - The Prayer of Jabez                     10

Day 5 - You Can't Stay There                    14

Day 6 - And So We Pray...                        19

Day 7 - The Products of Prayer                  22

Day 8 - Blurred Vision                          25

Day 9 - Don't Fight It – Part 1                 28

Day 10 - Don't Fight It – Part 2                31

Day 11 - Three Words    33

Day 12 - A Heart To Love Again    38

Day 13 - A Heart To Love Again…Again    41

Day 14 - Totally Covered    44

Day 15 - Miracles    47

Day 16 - Over-thinking    50

Day 17 - Before the Promise    53

Day 18 - Skipped    56

Day 19 - Silence    59

Day 20 - The Waiting Room    63

Day 21 - The Rain Came    68

Day 22 - Marathon    72

Day 23 - I Had To Sing…    76

Day 24 - 1, 2, 3 Sleeping    81

Day 25 - The Eye    84

Day 26 - Trust and Obey    88

Day 27 - The Yes Man    91

Day 28 - Don't Ask, Don't Tell                                         93

Day 29 - Saying and Doing                                              97

Day 30 - My Daughter                                                  99

Day 31 - Translation, Please                                      102

Day 32 - She Told Me                                              105

Day 33 - My Strength Came                                      107

Day 34 - Underground                                            110

Day 35 - Remembered                                          112

Day 36 - Shut In                                                114

Day 37 - No Air                                              116

Day 38 - He Promised                                        118

Day 39 - Favor Isn't Fair                                      120

Day 40 - The Rain Stopped                                  122

A Huge Thank You!!!                                          127

About Lydia Elle                                              129

# INTRODUCTION

*A*nd *So I Prayed...* is a devotional about getting through the storms of your life. It is about being in a place that God told you that you would *have* to go through in order to reach the life you want. Although He is definitive with the promise that He will deliver, that deliverance will come at the end of 40 days and nights of challenge and difficulty...and not before.

*And So I Prayed...* calls to the searching heart, the longing soul that wants to go deeper with God. My goal is not to call you to the beginning and end of a season of prayer, but rather to the start of a whole new chapter in life with Him. Prayer does not end on the fortieth day.

This book is not the end-all, be-all guide to how to go with God. Rather, it's a personal account of some of the key scriptures and promises that got me through my personal storm—my first 40-day season of prayer. I do not want you to copy me; actually, I think it is best that you don't. Your journey to this point is different from mine and your path with God going forward will be just as different. What I hope this book will do is encourage you to continue your journey, carry on with your search, and have faith that God will surely bring His promise to pass in your life. I want you to know that the rain *will* stop after 40 days, that you *will* make it through and that there is something amazing waiting for you when the storm is all over.

How do I know this? Because that is exactly what the Lord made happen for me.

DAY 1

# THE FIRST 40

*Go into the ark, you and your whole family, because I have found*
*you righteous in this generation…Seven days from now I will send*
*rain on the earth for forty days and forty nights, and I will wipe*
*from the face of the earth every living creature I have made.*
*(Genesis 7:1,4 NIV)*

can't tell you the first time I did a season of prayer. I have always known how important it is, but the power of prayer seemed fleeting in my life. That was probably a direct correlation to my faith in its power. I have been guilty of using God as a genie—of coming to Him asking for gifts and making requests as a last resort after I had done (or more often *not* done) all I was supposed to. I have fasted out of discipline, with the mindset that it is something I was supposed to do, but completely uncertain what I was supposed to get from it other than a growling stomach. I have come to prayer during my low times, groveling at the altar, but my sincerity was short-lived because as soon as my difficulties were behind me, so was my piety.

But then there came a time in my life that I wanted to be different. I *needed* my prayer experience to be different. And I knew there had to be something different. That was when I realized that my seasons of prayer did not exist in a vacuum. I needed to approach each one as a refreshing beginning.

1

My seasons of prayer and fasting were the doorway to the next level of myself, revealing to me what God wanted me to do, have and most important, be.

In my first 40 days I cried much more than I prayed. I hope that opening up about my storm and flood season will make it clear that you are not alone in your own feelings. There were nights that I thought I was going to die from heartbreak, lose my mind from all the stress, or suffocate from the confusion. Sometimes, I only wanted to sleep and never wake up. It was my winter time, not a season of unspeakable joy, indescribable happiness or clarity of purpose.

I recall nights of bitter loneliness, of tears burning my cheeks as they rolled down my face and of realizing that there was no one to wipe them away. Of functioning in a fog during the day, just wishing for the moment that I could crawl back into my bed and sleep through more time. On those occasions when I had to minister, I often wished I could forgo the requirement, knowing that my aching heart would reduce me to a sobbing heap of tears by the end of the song. During my first 40, it seemed that every time I had to sing, the song was a direct representation of all I was going through— God putting me on display as I inched my way through my perdition. But I kept praying—not always with words, but at least with my heart directed toward Him.

This book is a call to your heart, mind and soul to begin your search for God anew. To come to Him knowing that when you put your whole heart in His hand, you will find Him. This is not about religion, church, or a congregation, because you don't need any of those things to come before Him with your hope and humility. All you need to do is "draw nigh" to Him in your soul and I can testify that He will draw nigh unto you.

Yes, you may be broken. I was. Yes, this may be a time of trouble in your life. It was for me. Yes, the rains of distress may be raising you from the foundation you once knew as security and tossing you into the unknown. Been there. But just as He once promised to Noah, this is not a time that will end your journey, but rather the beginning of a whole new one.

These are the first 40 days of the rest of your life.

# DAY 2

# FEELINGS

*But the fruit of the Spirit is love, joy, peace, longsuffering, kindness, goodness, faithfulness, gentleness, self-control. Against such there is no law. (Galatians 5:22-23 NKJV)*

I could feel my spirit falling. At first, I heard just a few words: "No, he doesn't love you. He probably saw your call and doesn't want to talk to you. You will not be loved. You are not beautiful...just okay."

The enemy would whisper such things to me with the faintest of sounds, but he only had to do it for a few moments before I was repeating them to myself. I had *a lot* of insecurities about who I was, especially as my storm was raging, and I knew that I didn't want to be defined by my struggle, but I felt that it was all people could see when they looked at me. My solution? Hide from everyone.

To catch a thought before it becomes a feeling that determines an action is a skill of a lifetime. Thoughts are the seeds that produce the fruit: actions. I didn't have that skill yet. My emotions were anything but rational. It is true that I was dealing with a great deal, including things that other people had done to me, but I didn't have to give these situations and people so much control over my life. Yet I couldn't seem to grasp this. It was all so hard.

Being angry and not sinning was hard. Being hurt but not taking vengeance was hard. Being rejected and not retaliating was hard. I did not always take the high road. As my feelings were taken advantage of and I was taken for granted, I allowed others to have more control of my life than they should. I found myself swinging like a pendulum, unable to govern or predict my emotions for that day.

Then one Sunday morning, after praying, I heard God say this to me, as clear as day:

*If you are disappointed with how your life has turned out, don't complain about your harvest...check your seeds! You can't reap what you haven't sown."*

This hit me with such conviction I had to raise my hands in my kitchen and worship on the spot. It was what I was planting that was causing me to reap such anguish! And it wasn't just my seeds but the undernourished soil of my spirit that I was expecting to nurture them. I was giving friendship to those who only wanted my attention. I was giving love to people who only wanted to use me. I was giving money to things that would not provide a return. I was giving time to people who had no vested interest in my future. I sowed jealousy, doubt and lack of forgiveness (to name a few) but I didn't see that I was the one determining my harvest until God showed me.

*Don't complain about your harvest. Check your seeds.* Check your soil, and check your patience. Good seeds take time. Check to make sure they have water and light. Check the entire process of what you put forth into the world. Then be sure that you surrender your harvest to the God who makes all things grow.

Once God told me this and I realized that He had given me the power to change so many things in my life, I made the decision that day to do so. I recalibrated my outlook on life and how I viewed it through my emotions. I decided to pray daily about how I was feeling first instead of letting God know at the end of the day how I felt. This let me commit my mind to identifying where unproductive feelings were coming from. I would recall a promise from God that would either support my good feeling or block the bad one and recite it to myself throughout the day.

Before long, when the enemy would speak to me in his negative tone, I would shoot him down immediately with God's promises. I can't say that everything changed overnight or that every day was perfect; just like a crop of fruit, there were good ones and flawed ones. But over time, I did see a change that was sustainable…because I was relying on the One who could sustain me.

It would be a lie to say that I don't have a few down days or am not tempted to still doubt at weak moments. I do. But I can testify that I have a new outlook on my emotions. They do not control my faith. Now, it's the other way around.

# I WILL NEVER KNOW

*For I the LORD thy God will hold thy right hand, saying unto thee,*
*Fear not; I will help thee. (Isaiah 41:13 KJV)*

"**N**o thought can contain you, no idea can capture you.  So forgive me for my ignorance because even though I can say it, I'm truly unaware of all that you have done for me.  Though I may say thank you, I truly have no true idea of what 'everything' really is, but let me say it anyway... not because I know, but because I'm undoubtedly aware of the fact that I never will be..."

I remember when my heart said this to God in prayer.  It was late in the night and I was amazed at the idea that such Greatness would care about someone like me.  There are so many things that, if I were God, would seem so much more important. Sometimes, when I was caught up in my storm, I would feel like He was dealing with them instead of answering my prayers.  But then I'd recall this promise from Isaiah and be in awe that He would send me such a reminder.  God was (and is) on my team.  He truly believes in the purpose He has for my life, so much so that He has given me all that I need to accomplish it.  And if that's not a big enough deal, I am in awe of the fact that the God of the Universe actually listens to me when I call!  Whether in word or in my heart, He rushes to me before my heart even cries to Him.

One thing that kept me going through my 40-day storm was recalling how good God had already been to me in my life. From the time I was born, the enemy had been trying with all his might to either take my life or block me from living as God had planned. I didn't really think about the times my life had been spared, but as I began to pray this particular day it all came back to me and I realized in just how many ways God's majesty and splendor had touched my life.

There was one particular day, when I was about 6 years old and living in London. I was riding in the car with my aunt driving, my mother in the passenger seat, and my two cousins in the back seat with me. I was playing with the lock on the door as we were going up a hill. It was a main road and I remember looking out the window of the small car. My mother heard me playing with the lock on the door and told me to stop. I immediately heeded her instruction and stopped playing with the door, but just then my aunt made a right turn, my door flung open and I fell out of the moving car.

I began to roll down the street to the middle of this busy intersection—a major junction on a London motorway with three lanes of traffic going in either direction. But once I finished rolling, I stood up and looked around. I didn't see a car in sight! It was as though time was standing still. Then I saw my mother running towards me and, before I knew it, she had scooped me up in her arms. Panicked, she tried to make sure that I was okay, and my body flopped like a rag doll as I muttered, "Mummy, I'm okay." She walked with me back to the car, where my aunt was shaking with fear.

We continued driving, and my aunt drove with extreme caution. Everyone was silent. I had looked out the window a few seconds before the mishap and seen the hustle and bustle of busy London traffic. I knew that I should have been squashed under the wheel of a lorry or had a limb crushed under the weight of oncoming traffic. But nothing had happened. Every time I recalled the story, I was grateful for what God did in that situation, but after I prayed to Him in this moment, I realized that praise was due for so much more. God had saved me on that day in London, but this evening He brought to my attention that there was so much more He had saved me from that I will never know about.

This changed my whole perspective on God. His omnipresence and omniscience is not just about what I can fathom, but also all that I will never be able to fathom. I know Him to be the God of all that I know...but what I am truly grateful for, what He brought to my attention to help me through this night, is everything that I will *never know* He has done for me.

*God, You are amazing! You are all powerful! You are the only wise God. I worship You for all I know You have done and stand humbly acknowledging Your power and grace in saving me from dangers that I will never comprehend. I love You.*

# DAY 4

# THE PRAYER OF JABEZ

*Jabez was more honorable than his brothers. His mother had named him Jabez, saying, "I gave birth to him in pain." Jabez cried out to the God of Israel, "Oh, that you would bless me and enlarge my territory! Let your hand be with me, and keep me from harm so that I will be free from pain." And God granted his request.*
*(I Chronicles 4: 9-10 NIV)*

I was searching for answers about what to do next in my life when God placed this passage before me. I had heard it so many times before and really only looked at it as a text about money. And though money would have helped my situation in some regards, my life needed more than that. This was a middle of the night moment that kept me up till the wee hours of the morning. Here is what I learned that changed my life.

Many lessons can be drawn from the text. First, the history of Jabez himself should be understood. Though we are only given two verses to get to know him, a lot can be deduced from them—not only by what is said, but by all that is not said. The author is intentional in letting us know that Jabez was more "honorable" than his brothers. The word immediately suggests integrity, loyalty, strength, and dignity. It stands to reason that Jabez had brothers who were also honorable. The key to note is that while his brothers were upstanding, respected men in their community, Jabez stood out as the most respectable, with great honor and integrity based on his actions and what others saw in him.

Verse 10 shows us the prayer that Jabez utters. He asks God to bless Him and enlarge his territory. We do not know the reason why Jabez requested this of God, but we do know that he was a man of honor. Thus, it's likely that he would only ask for something that he needed, and it's equally likely that it would be used for more than his own personal gain. Because of Jabez' reputation, this was not a hard request for God to grant. His credit and honor had already been proven; he had shown that he was faithful. His track record of honor made God believe that Jabez would continue to be faithful and honorable if He granted his request, so God fulfilled it.

If we go back to verse 9, we get even more background. We learn that the name "Jabez" means 'born in pain.' Jabez was given this name by his mother, which in biblical times was the custom. A name was believed to represent the trademark character trait—the identity—of the person bearing it. The meaning of the name was not a secret, so calling a person by their name also meant that a particular thing was being spoken over them. This means that anyone saying or hearing the name Jabez would associate this name—and the person who bore it—with pain. And Jabez was given this name by his mother, the one who was supposed to love him the most! Jabez had to carry this weight for his entire life. So although he was honorable, even more so than all the other sons that his mother bore, he lived with a constant reminder that he was a source of pain.

The end of verse 10 addresses this point. Jabez asked God to keep him from evil so that he "may not cause pain." This seems like an odd and ill-placed request, given how honorable everyone knew him to be, but the truth is that he did not yet know he was honorable. No matter what he did, when people spoke his name he was reminded of his origin as a source of pain and suffering. It was because of the name his mother placed on him that he felt the need to cry to God for a release from what was holding him back. That would allow him to be fully effective in his new purpose.

This story—these two short verses—taught me so much that I was in tears. Its meaning and application in my life was revealed. The first lesson? *Credit.* Jabez asked for his territory to be enlarged and the blessing of increase. God granted this request without hesitation. Why? Because Jabez had been faithful. He had excellent credit with God, thus God extending him more credit was not a problem. The word territory in Hebrew is "gə·b̠ū·lî."[1] This word literally means 'border' or 'boundary.' In biblical times borders were contained using a rope. Thus, for Jabez to ask his territory to be enlarged, he was literally asking God to extend his rope. When my mother was a child walking to school, to carry her books she often had to secure them with a rope. The more books one had, the more rope one needed. The rope was directly proportional to the size of what was being carried and was just enough for the child carrying it to manage. As the child got stronger, he or she, could take on more weight. Sometimes, they needed a stronger rope to handle the greater weight.

Jabez had shown competence, honor and ability with the weight that he had been carrying. He had been responsible with the territory that he had, so when he asked God to enlarge his territory he knew that he would also need a longer rope and have to carry more weight. He was fine with this, and so was God.

The second lesson: *You do not have to let the name or title someone has given to you or your situation define who you are.* Someone else thinking you have reached the end of your story or written the finale of your legacy does not mean anything. God is the ultimate definer and coordinator of your life and can change what may look like a curse into a blessing. Jabez' mother gave him a name that reminded him every day that he was a source of great *pain.* But now when we

---

[1] James Strong, *The New Strong's Expanded Exhaustive Concordance of the Bible*, Expanded ed. (Nashville: Thomas Nelson, 2010)

think of Jabez, no one even realizes that. God redefined the legacy of Jabez to be what He had always planned on him becoming. Before this could happen, however, Jabez had to ask for a release from the mental, emotional and social chains that were binding him. His name, though it may have only been a word, was holding him back in the spiritual realm from becoming all that God had purposed for him to be. In his prayer he acknowledges this and asks that he no longer be able to 'cause pain.' The end of verse 10 says that God granted him his request—and the second request was far more important than the first. Jabez was now released to do *in God* because he was now known by God's definition *instead* of his mother's.

Even if God never gave Jabez anything more than the release of this pain, that would have been an awesome gift! But God saw fit to give him more. God gave him release from this spiritual and emotional chain and then enlarged his territory for him to use it. I truly pray that God finds me faithful with all I have, that he releases me from pain, and that he enlarges my territory not for my glory, but so I may continue to show others how great He is!

## DAY 5

# YOU CAN'T STAY THERE

*David and his men reached Ziklag on the third day. Now the Amalekites had raided Negev and Ziklag. They had attacked Ziklag and burned it, and had taken captive the women and everyone else in it, both young and old. They killed none of them, but carried them off as they went on their way. When David and his men reached Ziklag, they found it destroyed by fire and their wives and sons and daughters taken captive. So David and his men wept aloud until they had no strength left to weep. David's two wives had been captured—Ahinoam of Jezreel and Abigail, the widow of Nabal of Carmel. David was greatly distressed because the men were talking of stoning him; each one was bitter in spirit because of his sons and daughters. But David found strength in the LORD his God. Then David said to Abiathar the priest, the son of Ahimelek, "Bring me the ephod." Abiathar brought it to him, and David inquired of the LORD, "Shall I pursue this raiding party? Will I overtake them?" "Pursue them," he answered. "You will certainly overtake them and succeed in the rescue."*
*(1 Samuel 30: 1-9 NIV)*

*David recovered everything the Amalekites had taken, including his two wives. Nothing was missing: young or old, boy or girl, plunder or anything else they had taken. David brought everything back.*
*(1 Samuel 30:18 & 19 NIV)*

A song made popular in recent years by Donald Lawrence has one of my favorite voices singing lead, Ms. Sheri Moffet Jones. This powerful song, on more than one occasion, has caused me to pull over in my car and shout in praise. All I need is to hear the first line and I am in exultation:

*"Some — times - you have to encourage yourself..."*

The idea that you could lift yourself up in the Lord was so powerful for me during my 40 days that I would often cry in desperation for such relief.

I read the passage from 1 Samuel after praying about some friendships that were strained and lost during my storm. I didn't understand why I had lost them or even what to do next. The pain was so real that I wanted to stay away from anything that might cause similar grief. As I talked with God about this, however, He told me that I was not allowed to remain in that space; I couldn't stay reclusive and hidden. Despite the pain that I felt, I still had a purpose to accomplish. I could not allow myself to be blinded by the distress that others were causing in my life.

The story of David and his men in 1 Samuel 30 is a powerful one and it's the basis for this song, I'm sure. Often I was stuck on the idea of encouraging myself. But how the Bible presents this idea is key, because it showed me that the power to change my feelings is within myself. I have been guilty of trying to excuse my attitude or mishaps on my circumstances or my feelings about them, saying that my reckless ways should be excused because I was discouraged. But this story paints a completely different picture.

In Scripture, David had gone to the Philistine camp to seek refuge and safety from King Saul. The king of the Philistines, King Achish, and David made an agreement that he would be safe with them as long as he became a part of the Philistine army. David agreed to these terms and King Achish gave David and his men the city of Ziglag as a place for them and their families to dwell safely. Soon the Israelites under Saul's leadership came up against the Philistines and war was imminent. The Philistine army did not trust that David and his men would be loyal to them and advised the king to throw them out. So King Achish sent a message to David and his men while they were readying themselves for battle against the Israelites that they would have to leave Philistine territory.

David and his men traveled for three days from the Philistine camp back to Ziglag. When they arrived, they found their town burned to the ground and their wives and children taken captive. David and his men wept together until they had no more strength to weep. In Verse 6 the story takes a pivotal turn and says that after this weeping that the men had done together David became greatly distressed because his men were talking of stoning him. However, "David encouraged himself in the Lord his God." He then asked God if he and his men should go after the Amalekites and rescue his loved ones. God said yes, and the story ended with David rescuing all who were taken captive.

There are three lessons from this story that taught me about encouragement and that God used to fortify me from that point to now. The first is that there *will* (not might) come a time that the very people you have fought with, traveled rough roads with and suffered with will abandon you. David's men were so distraught about the loss of their families and the devastation of their property that they could not see past their own grief to realize that they were misguided about its source. Because they had sided with David for his cause, they felt that he was to blame for their loss. They no longer were a part of the same team, because they could only see their individual situations.

God showed me that I should not hold on to the rejection that those I called friends were directing my way because they could only see their own situations. As much as this hurt, this revelation made it easier to handle rejection and still pray for my friends.

The next lesson: the Bible says that all the women and children had been carried away. So when David's friends turned on him, the expected support from family was not there. The lesson here is that there *will* also come a time when those who you call family will not be able to help you in your situation— not because they don't want to, but because of some bondage they are experiencing in their own lives. During my storm my family did their best to be supportive, but because they were not where I was, they couldn't understand all I was going through. I found myself constantly trying to explain my feelings, my pain and my decisions to the point of exhaustion. But when God showed me that I could not hold this against them but rather give them the time to deal with their own burdens, it became much easier to deal with.

With all of this there is hope in darkness. Although everyone was taken captive from the town, the Bible says that no one was killed. God showed me that this meant what had been taken from me would be restored. My source of strength would be restored. There was, however, work to do.

The famous passage from this chapter speaks to David encouraging himself in the Lord. I found this to be amazing. To think that I could get all I needed by just speaking life over my situation and myself! It was then that I asked God for strength to speak in a positive manner about where I was and where I needed to go. I asked Him to help me stay strong despite the demolition of my life, and I pleaded with Him to keep me encouraged. I was able to find joy in the little things: the sun shining, helping someone else or just somebody sending me an encouraging text. Because I was doing my best to stay encouraged in God, He began to flood me with encouragement. Just speaking with Him, instead of rehearsing my problems with others, made me feel much better.

There is a key part to the David story that I have not yet covered. After David encouraged himself, he realized that he still had work to do and "inquired of the Lord" as to how to proceed. Many times we speak of this time of encouragement and want to get comfortable there. This place is only a season you are to pass through so that you can continue to do what you have been called to do. If David had just stayed at the level of encouraging himself instead of moving to action, he never would have gotten back all that he had lost or even been ready for next phase in his leadership

When David inquired of the Lord as to whether he would find victory if he attacked the Amalekites, God told him to proceed. David took the time he needed to gain strength, but then he knew that he had to go and get back all that was taken. When he went to get his family back, the Bible says that not one person was killed and that he recovered every single thing that was taken, not just for himself but for all his men.

As much as I sometimes want to stay in private praise with God, getting encouragement and strength, it would mean nothing for me if I didn't use my testimony and voice to propel me to fulfill my purpose. Singing in my shower was not what He has called me to do. He wants me to sing in front of thousands. Speaking only with Him about my pain was not what He wanted me to do. Rather, He has charged me with sharing how I overcame my painful moments through Him so that others may be encouraged that the same can come to pass in their lives. As much as I wanted to stay in that place of encouragement with God, He needed me in battle so that those around me who are lost would not let grief blind them to the need for action. God told me, even with the rain pouring down, that I could get the encouragement I needed from Him, but then there was work to be done.

DAY 6

# And So We Pray...

*The effectual and fervent prayer of a righteous man availeth much.*
*(James 5:16 KJV)*

*The prayer of a righteous person is powerful and effective.*
*(James 5:16 NIV)*

*The prayer of a person living right with God is something powerful to be reckoned with.*
*(James 5:16 TMB)*

*The earnest (heartfelt, continued) prayer of a righteous man makes tremendous power available (dynamic in its working).*
*(James 5:16 AMP)*

I had to write this Scripture in a few different versions, because if you are anything like me you may have wondered what makes prayer work. There are countless stories in the bible of great men and women speaking to God and Him granting their request immediately. There are other times, as with Hannah, where a child of the king would have to petition for what seemed like an eternity before their request was granted. There are other times still, like with David, in which God did not grant the request.

During my stormy period I prayed what seemed like a million prayers. I prayed in agony, in trouble, in hurt, in pain, in frustration, in fear, and in worry. I prayed when I was happy, when I thought things were too good to be true, when I didn't believe that what was coming to me would be possible, and when I was tired. There were many, many tired moments. It is only looking back now that I see that the 'working' of prayer is not really about the answer, but the progress and power that I received in the process.

If I asked for healing, then when I got off my knees, I felt powerful belief that Who I just spoke to had all power in His hands. If I prayed for a financial blessing, I felt fortified to know that even if He didn't send what I requested, everything would be taken care of. If I prayed for comfort, when I finished I would feel like the Creator of the universe had stopped all He was doing to come off His throne and give me a hug. What I realized is that I wasn't always given the answer I was looking for, but I definitely received the one I needed.

What is the purpose of prayer? Continued prayer keeps our mind focused in the right place. In prayer, our focus leaves what is around us and ascends heavenward. God is able to open our eyes to what He has for us beyond what we can see, and thus what we see no longer causes the stress and worry that it used to. The prayers that I prayed during my lonely moments allowed me to focus on where my help comes from and put my faith back into the place it needed to be.

*"The (continued) prayer of a righteous man..."*

When we are continual with prayer, we are drawn closer to the One we are talking to. The relationship between us and our ultimate Friend is strengthened because we are spending more time together. Whenever you spend more time with someone you get more comfortable around them. I didn't do much dating during my storm, but I would be lying if I said I didn't daydream about it. When I think of a developing relationship with someone,

I think of the time that we have to share the details of our lives. It is in the sharing and listening that we grow closer and develop a bond that gets stronger over time. Without communication, the relationship would be hollow and probably wouldn't last. It takes time, attention and intention to ensure that there is a connection between people. I have friends that I talk to once a year, and we can pick right back up like no time has passed at all, but it is quality and trust that maintains those bonds.

The relationship I have with my daughter has truly taught me about trust. She trusted me from the moment that she saw me, because she had no choice. However, as I kept proving myself to her, her trust in me kept growing. The trust that she has developed for me over the last five years is there today because of experience. Her experience with me in her past gives her total confidence in me for the future. I believe it is for this reason why God says that we should be as little children—because their trust is total and complete from birth.

Prayer is not first about the revelation of the answer—but rather for the realization of Who we are talking to.

# The Products of Prayer

*The effectual and fervent prayer of a righteous man availeth much.*
*(James 5:16 KJV)*

*The prayer of a righteous person is powerful and effective.*
*(James 5:16 NIV)*

*The prayer of a person living right with God is something powerful to*
*be reckoned with.*
*(James 5:16 TMB)*

*The earnest (heartfelt, continued) prayer of a righteous man makes*
*tremendous power available (dynamic in its working).*
*(James 5:16 AMP)*

As I prayed in the darkest moments of my life, I found that my prayers were producing many more products than I was asking for. Honesty was one. Because I was coming to God desperate to speak about how I was truly feeling, for my prayers to be effective I had to face the situations with a somber realism that would not allow me to hide behind pretense and the "I'm fine" lie that I told so many people. I soon learned that honesty in prayer was not to inform God of how I was feeling (as though He didn't know about my situation, or I could hide it), but rather so that I would finally face it.

There were so many secrets that I often was trying to keep them hidden from myself. But until I actually faced them, surrendered them to God and forgave myself for them, instead of trying to bury them, I would not get past them. The thing about a secret struggle is that most of its power lies not in the actual secret but in the effort you have to put forth to keep it as such. It took all my time and energy to convince myself that I was okay with all that I was carrying around and trying to manage on my own. Finally, when I presented it all to God in its raw form, in the middle of my storm and my pain, I felt lighter. I knew that Someone knew the real me and still loved me. It was in this space and freedom that the second product of prayer came to light.

The products of prayer, at least in my experience:

1.  *Peace.* (Isaiah 23:6) Because I was talking to God so often and in such an intimate way, I no longer had time to dwell on the things that had been stealing my opportunity for peace. The continuing conversation I had with Him throughout the day about my fears, as I looked at certain situations and faced certain people, began to fade. Because we were talking so much and so often, I stopped wanting to talk about the problems I wanted Him to fix in my life and began to talk about the future that I knew He had planned for me once the rain was over.

    There was such joy in the hope of what was to come that the rain falling all around me changed from weights on my heart to refreshing renewal. I knew that all that I once was I would be no longer. All He wanted me to be was taking shape. I still had to go through each and every day of my forty days' deluge, but there were days that the rain felt lighter because I knew He was with me...sheltering me. I could accept the rain for its purpose and allow the current of His will to guide my heart and mind. Prayer allows us to be so comfortable in a storm that we can sleep as Jesus did. Not because the storm isn't disrupting our lives, but because the internal peace is greater than the external destruction.

My relationship with God grew in our moments together, so much so that when I faced the same troubles again I no longer had the same reaction. I knew, due to my relationship and continued communication with Jesus; that with all that He had done before He would certainly get me through what was to come.

Prayer may not always mean deliverance. Sometimes, it is a means of showing God that we trust him implicitly, and that whatever He sees fit to do in our situation will be for our ultimate best and bring Him glory...*and* we will be fine with that. It is better to be suffering in His will than enjoying pleasure outside of it.

2. *Power.* "Prayer...availeth much." The power that came into my life as I turned to prayer was undeniable. I felt powerful because I knew I had God on my side and based all my faith on knowing that all things could be done through Him. We unleash the power of God in our lives once we surrender our lives through honesty, trust Him implicitly and receive peace. He will do just what He has promised to do.

Power does not come from getting God to do our will, but standing behind Him believing that He will perform His will in our life. We will have nothing to fear about where we going, what He is doing or how He will do it. All we need to do is pray about everything and stand on the promise that He is going to handle every situation in the best way possible for us.

# Blurred Vision

*For we walk by faith, not by sight. (2 Corinthians 5:7 ESV)*

I was a broken mess. I felt like a walking heap of tears ready to detonate at a moment's notice. I did my best to dress up and put on a little makeup everyday, but inside I was dying. I was yearning for someone, anyone, to reach out to me. Church no longer gave me the 'high' I needed because what I was dealing with was more than a quick hug and a "how are you?" could fix. I needed healing. It had only been three months since I had begun my storm and though there was peace on one level as I knew God has said this would happen, there was much unrest on many others. I was wrestling with God to get answers about what He wanted me to do next. Of course, as I always did, I mistakenly gave Him suggestions, but I felt like I wasn't moving forward. I was just going in circles as to what my next move should be and He wasn't giving me any direction.

Webster's defines a storm as "A disturbance of the atmosphere marked by wind and usually by rain, snow, hail, sleet, or thunder and lightning."

When God told Noah that He would send a flood for 40 days and 40 nights, I'm sure that Noah imagined what God was speaking of. But because a flood had never actually happened before, Noah really didn't know what he was preparing the ark for. When I entered into the process of my divorce, I had an idea of what was about to happen, but I honestly did not have the slightest idea of what the experience would be like or how it would make me feel. I was sure that it would be hard and there would be moments when I would question everything, but it was completely different once I was actually in the middle of it.

But God needed to disturb my atmosphere. He needed to change and remove all that I had faith in so that my faith would look up to Him. I had done so much that I had *thought* was coming from faith, but that was born of need or vanity. I had sung an astounding number of songs over the years, but they had no real meaning until my own moments of flooding came upon me. On innumerable occasions, I had gotten down on my knees to pray, but I had not truly capitalized on the opportunity to open my heart. I could see all that could happen in theory, but it wasn't until He blurred my vision that I could really see Him with my faith.

Did I mention that I was a broken mess? My heart was anything but intact and I was crying out constantly for salvation that only God could provide. I tried other people and experiences, but they did not reach me during my storm the way that I needed: giving me true reassurance that everything was going to be all right. And so, during my storm I did things that pulled me further away from God. Yet each choice always gave me nothing more than additional brokenness and unanswered questions. I finally turned to God and said:

"My life is like a window pane. Glass that, based on things that I have brought on myself or that have been done to me, has been broken. So in my need to control and fear of trusting I have picked up all the pieces of my brokenness and held on to them as tight as I can for fear of being hurt again. Though I say I trust You completely, I have only trusted You with pieces of my life and expected You to put them back together." But God told me that He can't put them back together unless He has everything. With all the other pieces in my hand, I have either held them so tightly that they have cut me or given them to someone else who could never have put them back together and who returned them more broken than before.

What happens when you hold tightly to broken glass? You cut yourself. I was hurting myself even more as I tried to keep it together, trying to hold on and deal with the pain that continued to cut deeper and deeper. I looked to find people who would heal me, but they did not have the power. Then He said it: "Lydia, let go." That night I got down on my knees and said "God, I'm sorry. I trust You more than I trust me." I let go of everything: my job, my worries, my hurt, my fears, my pain, my daughter, and my life. I let it all go and began my journey to trust God.

I could barely see what was in front of me...but I realized later that I didn't need to see. Through this storm I was not walking by sight, but by faith, and He needed my vision to be blurry so that I would not try to lean on what I was seeing and make decisions about my next steps, but lean on Him.

All along, I thought the rain that fell on me was just part of my storm. But while God could have cleansed the earth in a different way, instead of sending a flood, rain is what He chose. Finally, I think I know why. Just as Noah and his family couldn't see everything that was happening outside because the waters covered it, the rain was put in my life so that I couldn't see too. I had to trust God. Now I can say I am thankful for my blurred vision.

DAY 9

# DON'T FIGHT IT - PART 1

*Now a man named Lazarus was sick. He was from Bethany, the
village of Mary and her sister Martha. (This Mary, whose brother
Lazarus now lay sick, was the same one who poured perfume on the
Lord and wiped his feet with her hair.) (John 11:1-2 NIV)*

Because I grew up in England, one of the things I had to learn quickly upon
moving to Canada was that the names of some things in England were
not exactly the same in Canada. Despite the fact that both countries speak
English, I quickly realized that things were not identical. I am a British girl,
born at King's College Hospital right into my grandmother's hands. I have
so many wonderful memories of my childhood in London. Memories like
playing on the swings with my friends and making daisy necklaces and grass
rings. I loved getting sweets from the local corner store with the 10p my
mom or dad would give me on Sunday morning. When I was eight years
old my parents decided that our family would migrate to Canada in pursuit
of opportunity. Even at a young age I was excited about all the possibilities
the unknown would bring and embraced the idea of living in a new country.

One of my first experiences with this came while my mother and I were
on the bus one day. I was trying to learn the new language of Canada, since
there were so many words that I had to learn. A few examples:

In England, a treat was a sweet. In Canada, it was called candy.
In England, we sat on the loo. In Canada, we sat on the toilet.
In England, the toilet was the room where we found the loo. In
Canada, that was the washroom.

There were some embarrassing mistakes. While on the bus one day, we were
passing by a group of apartments. In England, apartments like this are called
'flats' and I knew they were called condominiums, but I couldn't remember
the short form of the word. So, to try and sound like I was acclimating well
to my new country, I said,

"Mum, those are condoms, right?"

People looked and snickered, and I immediately felt embarrassed. My
mother quickly hushed me and replied, "No dear, they are condos, not
condoms."

Another word that made people look at me like I was crazy was "queue."
In London when you were at the bank or waiting in the pharmacy and you
were not sure of where the line started you would ask the person who you
thought was at the end, "Excuse me, are you in the queue?" The first time
I asked someone that in my third grade class, I was laughed at for the rest of
the day (what made it worse was that I had asked with a thick British accent).

What does this have to do with Lazarus? Bear with me. The story of
Lazarus is by far one of Jesus's most praised miracles. It was the knowledge
of what Jesus did for Lazarus that caused the Pharisees much displeasure.
They wanted to erase all record that his resurrection even happened. What
God told me about this story, though, was the process that Lazarus had to go
through before his resurrection even happened.

Lazarus was the brother of Mary and Martha and a close friend of Jesus.
He had hosted Jesus in his home on numerous occasions as the Lord traveled

though Bethany to other towns and cities. He had talked with Jesus and dined with him, spoken with him about his goals and dreams, seen him heal the sick and give people hope in their darkest of situations. When Lazarus got sick, it stands to reason that he would believe that his friend, whom he had seen do so many amazing things, would heal him, too.

It soon became clear that Lazarus' sickness was more than home remedies could handle. The Bible says that his sisters sent word to Jesus to come and help, but Jesus did not come. Imagine how Lazarus must have felt? As the pain wracked his body, as he writhed in agony, he never saw Jesus come to his aid. It was as though his request was put in the queue, like when you call customer service and are told that your call will be answered in the order in which it was received. It doesn't matter whether it was in the front of the line or the middle—all Lazarus knew was that Jesus was not attending to his great need, even though he knew the Lord had the power to heal him.

In my darkest of moments when I saw no answers, heard no voice and felt no difference, I also felt as though my Friend had abandoned me. I had known Him to do so much for others and fix their issues, so why would He not fix mine? This was one of my hardest moments in the storm. I didn't see why God wouldn't just fix my situation immediately. It was not an easy situation and I did not handle it gracefully. I coughed and choked on the bad choices that had gotten me to that place, sneezed on the wrongs done to me, and gagged on the hurt that people's actions caused me. I was so confused.

My prayer during this time was simple: *God I don't understand. I don't know what to do and I don't think I will make it through this.* But, as with Lazarus, he didn't expect me to. He wanted me to keep talking to Him and trusting that His plans to heal me were better than my ideas for fixing my situation. I didn't trust well in this moment, but I tried. Looking back now, I wish I had done better, but that was a lesson too.

## DAY 10

# DON'T FIGHT IT - PART 2

*So the sisters sent word to Jesus, "Lord, the one you love is sick."*
*(John 11:3)*

At some point, Lazarus must have realized he was going to die. He must have realized that Jesus wasn't coming to help him, and he must have been totally lost as to why any of this was happening to him.

To say that I have been there is an understatement. There were relationships that I realized God was not going to save. Jobs that God was going to block me from getting. Promotions He was going to deny me from receiving. I had been trying to save so many things in my life, things that I prayed and begged God would help me keep, but as I tried to grasp them with all of my will, I watched in horror as God allowed the life to be drained from those relationships, situations and opportunities.

Webster's defines "quandary" as a "state of perplexity or doubt" or "being in a difficult situation." As one cherished part of my life after another sickened and died, I found myself confused as to why God would let that happen to me. I doubted whether He really knew best. Why wouldn't he want my relationship to work? Why wouldn't he want me to get the better job I'd

31

been trying for? Why wouldn't he want me to thrive? Why would he want these bad things to happen to me?

It didn't make sense. It made it hard to pray, hard to praise, and hard to trust. I wanted to, but I felt life leaving all that I thought I was living for. The death of the life I had been trying to build felt imminent.

I almost crumbled under the pressure. With the clear response of "wait" that I knew Jesus uttered in response to my desperate prayer, I faced the certainty that my sickness was going to end in death. But it was a kind of death—and a kind of rebirth—that I could not have anticipated.

You know the outcome of Lazarus' story. Jesus raised him from the dead and he was reborn in Christ. The same had to happen to my old life, and there was suffering along the way. There always is when something dies. There are situations in our lives that we are asking God to heal because they are sick, but He has decided that those things need to die in our life so He can resurrect in us an even better life than before. Sickness and death are not necessarily the end of your life, but the pause before He resurrects a brighter future for you. While you are going through your own storm, do not ever think that the Father does not see, know or have a plan for you. Remember that His thoughts are so much higher than our thoughts and His ways are higher than our ways. We may not see the plan, but it does not mean that He does not have one.

DAY 11

# THREE WORDS

*Shortly before dawn Jesus went out to them, walking on the lake.*
*When the disciples saw him walking on the lake, they were terrified.*
*"It's a ghost," they said, and cried out in fear.*
*But Jesus immediately said to them: "Take courage! It is I.*
*Don't be afraid."*
*"Lord, if it's you," Peter replied, "tell me to come to you on the water."*
*"Come," he said. Then Peter got down out of the boat, walked on*
*the water and came toward Jesus. But when he saw the wind, he*
*was afraid and, beginning to sink, cried out, "Lord, save me!"*
*Immediately Jesus reached out his hand and caught him. "You of*
*little faith," he said, "why did you doubt?" And when they climbed*
*into the boat, the wind died down. Then those who were in the boat*
*worshiped him, saying, "Truly you are the Son of God."*
*(Matthew 14:25-33 NIV)*

My storm got so strong that I was often tempted to think that I would not make it. That I would never get out of it. That the rain would never stop. I felt like the weight I carried would crush my spirit and leave me a shell of who I am—going through the motions of life but not living it. Often I would try to pray to God and though I knew what to say, I couldn't say it with the life or faith that it needed to go any further than the ceiling. My heart was not in it.

If nothing else, remember that no matter what you say in prayer, what is most important is that you feel what you are saying. One word or ten thousand—if there is no feeling behind it then you are just speaking to yourself.

In Scripture, Peter, found himself walking towards the very One who had the power to let Him do so. The reason He was on the water with the Lord was because He needed proof. I often need proof that God is really listening. He and I have a constant communication flow, yet there are times when He will speak to me and I am unsure that it is really Him on the other end of the line. I have found, however, that the moments when I am most unsure are the moments when He tells me to do the very thing I have asked Him if I should do. Often, it's been a crazy request. Peter didn't say to Jesus "Lord, if it really you then tell me how the weather is right now." A request like that isn't going to change anyone in spirit.

In our prayers we are often guilty of making requests that are meaningless: "Lord, if it is you, tell me not to eat this doughnut." I love sweets, so the Lord telling me to not eat the doughnut is not really necessary; I know I should not be eating it! What Peter asked was for God to do the impossible—*something that He could only do if He was God!* This test called not only for proof but required action on Peter's part.

"Lord, if it's you…tell me to come to you on the water."

I don't know if Peter was thinking when he made this request. He may not have realized that while he was demanding action of Jesus, more important action would be required of himself. All Jesus had to do was say, "Come." What Peter was required to do was a bit more…challenging.

The boat that Peter was in was not on the shore at the time. At that moment the disciples were crossing the lake. Earlier that day they had seen Jesus perform one of His greatest miracles, feeding the 5000, and He told them to go ahead while He went to the mountain to pray. On the heels of such an experience, they were probably in awe. To see the multiplicative power of His hands must have been one of the focal points in their conversation that night. But Jesus told them to go ahead. As the disciples were floating to the other side of the lake, they remembered that Jesus had left for the mountainside. Thus, when they saw Him on the water, they were completely surprised. This is why they likened Him to a ghost. If the disciples had thought it possible for Jesus to meet them, they would not have been afraid when they actually saw Him.

I have been guilty of leaving Jesus where He performed my last miracle, not realizing that He is with me during my moments of transition. As I travel from one place to another, I sometimes forget that He is with me wherever I go. Then I, too, become afraid when I see Him again, because I do not recognize Him. When God completes a miracle in your life, it is fine to speak of the miracle, but do not get so hung up on the act that you forget about His presence in your life's transitions.

First, Peter had to get out of the boat. I don't know if Peter really thought about what He was asking Jesus to do or what Jesus would ask of him. The boat was his only mode of transportation, so to leave the boat was to leave his only way of getting from one side of the lake to the other. But because he wanted to have proof of who Jesus was, he had to abandon what was in his power and risk something that could only be achieved under the power of Another. When God calls you to come, you will be required to leave what you know to be tried and true to do something that looks impossible. Why? It is to show you that what you desire your life to be can only be done with God's power instead of your own.

Once Peter got out of the boat, his test was not done. The next thing he had to do was move toward Jesus. He had to walk. Often times I have had enough faith to get out of my situation, but am so paralyzed by the idea of doing it that I haven't been able to move. Jesus said "Come" and a big part of Peter's test was to see if he could do what he saw Jesus doing. Jesus had been walking on the water towards them, which was what started the whole commotion in the first place. Peter wanted to see if Jesus could give him the power to do the same thing. Because Jesus wasn't standing still, neither could Peter. For all that God has called us to be, we must resist the urge to stay in one place. We must move into our destiny, purpose and future, even if it seems that we are walking on the waters of total and unadulterated impossibility. We must move.

It is during the moving that we must have the most faith. It was here that Peter began to lose his faith. Peter began to walk on the water just as he had seen Jesus do. However, as he began to walk on the water "He saw the wind." I have seen what wind can do in a storm; it can be unnerving. I have seen it push rain in one direction or another. I have seen it blow leaves down the street and bend trees to the point that it looks like they will break. But I have never actually *seen* the wind. Now, the Bible does not tell us that Peter looked at the water and began to sink. It does not mention that he looked down at all. Much as I would like to believe that he lost faith as he realized the impossibility of what he was doing, I can't say that is true. What I think actually happened is that Peter became distracted by something that he couldn't even see. He saw the wind and became afraid. So he saw something that *could not be seen* and allowed that to sow a seed of doubt and take root in Him.

As I write this, I think of all the times that I have been moving according to God's instruction and allowed myself to become distracted by other people's "what ifs" and "are you sures?" By allowing other people's doubts to make me doubt, I have become afraid. Totally forgetting the fact that I am actually walking on impossibility, I get distracted by something invisible that I think I can see, and I sink into what I had been walking on with confidence.

However, I have good news. When Peter was sinking into the water as he walked to Jesus, he did not have time for an elaborate prayer. His cry to God at this moment encapsulated all the elements that prayer needs: a heart turned towards God and a sincere sentiment.

Jesus told Peter to come and he was still trying to do so, even though he was sinking. When we pray to God we must remember that turning our hearts to Him, ensuring that we focus on Him alone in those moments, sets us up for the deliverance that is to follow. Peter did this, and He prayed a prayer of the utmost sincerity, crying out, "Lord, save me." Prayer needs this kind of sincerity. It cannot be bashful, timid or lofty so that we do not present our true heart's petitions to God. He wants to know the real things within us. Once we open our hearts to Him, He will give us the Hand we need to deliver us from our situation. Don't think that Jesus didn't see Peter sinking before he said something. But Peter had to *decide* that he wanted Jesus to save him.

Give your sincere and heartfelt burdens to God. Do not tell Him what you think He wants to hear, but tell him what you know you must. It is at this moment that you will find the immediate Hand of deliverance. He is already there waiting to save you. You do not have to do anything to aid in your own rescue but decide you want to be saved and call on Him.

# DAY 12

# A Heart To Love Again

*...Love never gives up. Love cares more for others than for self. Love doesn't strut. Doesn't force itself on others. Doesn't fly off the handle. Doesn't keep score of the sins of others. Doesn't revel when others grovel. Puts up with anything. Always looks for the best. Never looks back, but keeps going to the end.*
*(1 Corinthians 13:3-7 MSG)*

I'm no expert in love. I have failed at showing it, failed at believing in it and failed at choosing where I thought I could find it. Not long ago, I came to the conclusion that all my failures with love were due to two causes:

1. My lack of understanding.
2. Looking for it in the wrong place.

The first recollection I have of love was from my mother. She loved me in a way that enveloped all that I was. Growing up, I knew that she loved me and she was very active in showing it. Her love didn't always come with grand gestures (though I will never forget my surprise seventh birthday party when I got my first pair of blue roller skates), but it's little things that I remember the most, like walking to the bakery holding her hand, and her letting me buy a sweet for 5p while she picked up some essentials for the house.

We had something so special that it has stayed with me, and each memory makes me smile.

My mother, however, was not able to show me how a man should love me. By no fault of her own, I did not have a strong father figure in my life. This made it hard to comprehend and accept my Heavenly Father's love for me. Looking back now, I see this was a ploy of the enemy to sever all possibility of my knowing God for myself. Because I didn't understand the love of a man or a father, I didn't know what to expect from one or even to admit that I needed it.

The decisions I made during my dating years all manifested the fact that I was never exposed to this love. All my life I had been taught that God loved me, but I grappled everyday with the practical nature of that concept. How could God love me when so many others that I had begged to do just that decided to walk away from me? How could God love me when every day I struggled just to like myself? How could God love me with all that I had done wrong in my life? I didn't feel that I had just made mistakes; I often felt that I actually *was* one. How could God love me?

My pregnancy was one of the worst experiences in my life. From the time I was six weeks along until the day my daughter was born, I vomited violently and consistently every day. I didn't sleep well. I was always dehydrated. My throat was raw and my energy was pretty much non-existent. Everything was a trigger for my nausea and I couldn't keep any food down. During the months as I grew bigger I knew that the end was in sight, but I was depressed and crying about how terrible this process was. The people around me didn't understand the extent to which I was suffering. Many who didn't have firsthand experience belittled and dismissed my symptoms. I felt so isolated and alone during this time, even from my husband. I would visit the hospital almost every week to get intravenous fluids but as soon as I returned home I would start vomiting again. I honestly thought it would never end.

But then my daughter was born. I remember looking down at her and instantly feeling incredible love. It was so deep and so natural that I was overwhelmed. I knew that this little person depended on me for everything and I didn't feel burdened by the responsibility, but rather privileged to be granted it. It was at this moment that I finally, *finally* understood love.

When my daughter was born, I became her mother. It wasn't something that I had to do, or work to be, but rather just inherent to me because of her existence. Because she existed, I was now a mother. And my loving her was who I was. It was as I looked down at her little face and tiny hands that I realized I could never fathom how much God loved me. My thoughts were if I was totally engulfed in loving her as much as I do and I am human, then God's love for me *had* to be incalculable. That morning, at 4:30am and after eight hours of labor, I thanked God that He loved me…and that I could finally have a glimpse of what that meant.

## DAY 13

# A HEART TO LOVE AGAIN...AGAIN

*God is love. (I John 4:8 KJV)*

This letter I wrote to God captures the pain I was in during part of my storm:

*Jesus, I am worn out from crying. How did I get here again? Why is it that someone won't want to love me and keep me? I try to give so much and it seems that whatever I give is not good enough. I don't think I am strong enough to lose any more. To have to watch the person you love walk away because they love someone else...Lord, I just can't take it. My heart is beyond broken; it is dust. I don't even recognize the pieces of who I am to try and put it back together.*

*I have friends who tell me to be cold and just do what I want, but what I want is to be loved. To be loved and kept. To be enough for someone. I know that you love me, but you know that I can go for days without human contact. And Lord, I love you with all I am, but I am begging you to send me more or please help me to no longer desire this. Better yet, can you just come down here and give me a hug? All I need right now is a hug and the reminder that everything is going to be all right.*

*I want to get to the place where you are enough for me. I want to know I can make it through these moments with just a prayer to you. This is why I am telling you first. I ask that you please help my loneliness, please heal my brokenness and please, please, please let me feel your love today. I don't just want it, I need it to make it through. I love you with all the pieces that I am...*

*Lydia*

1 John 4.8 sums everything up: *"God is love."*

Love is not something that God has to work to be or do. Because He is love, He cannot do anything else but love us. Therefore, I never had to look for His love in my life, for the mere fact that I existed meant that He loved me (remember Chapter 12). He has said that He loves us with an everlasting love, which means that when I cease to live on this earth, He will still love me because I was here. I will love my daughter forever and ever. No matter what she does, where she goes, or what mistakes she makes. I will love her always, because she is mine, and I will forever be her mother.

Thus, the love that I needed in my life, to fill the emptiness and clear the misunderstanding I had of it, could only be found in Jesus. This meant that what I had been longing for from people—specifically from men—could only come from Him. All this time I had been doing the people in my life a disservice with my expectations. How could I expect a perfect love from an imperfect person? It was too much for them to carry and too much for me to put on them. I had to learn this lesson the hard way...a few times over.

I didn't fully accept the love of God until I was well into my storm. I'd had glimpses of acceptance, but because I felt so bad about myself, I didn't feel that anyone should be allowed to get close enough to love me. However, one night, as I lay in my bed, I prayed a prayer like this:

*God, I'm so tired. My heart is so tired. My eyes are tired. My spirit is tired. I don't understand why those who I desire to love me do not love me and I cannot take any more heartache. Could you please fix it? Please?*

His response to me was simple and easy that night. "I love you tired or with energy. I love you when you understand it and when you don't. I love you when you love yourself and when you punish yourself. I loved you all this time, even before you loved yourself. It wasn't that I needed your permission to love you, but you needed to let yourself see it to realize that I always have and always will. Now rest, honey. Just rest."

The day I realized this, I could not help but love Him back. Yes, Jesus loves me. I know this because He told me so.

# DAY 14

# TOTALLY COVERED

*They rose greatly on the earth, and all the high mountains under the entire heavens were covered. The waters rose and covered the mountains to a depth of more than fifteen cubits. (Genesis 7:19-20 NIV)*

When I have thought of mountains in the past, I referred to the many sermons I encountered that used them as analogies. They were the seemingly insurmountable problems, people or blockages that had to be passed before I got to the promised destination. Usually, the lesson was accompanied by the story of Jesus in which He told His disciples that if they had as much faith as a mustard seed, they would be able to speak to the mountain and tell it to be moved. (Matt 17:20, Luke 17:6). But let's think about mountains for a minute...

Recently I took a trip to California and my friend drove me along the coast. It was absolutely beautiful! If there is one thing that I unequivocally love, it is the ocean. It calms my mind and puts my entire body at rest. Then he said that we were going to turn and drive through the mountains to get back home. The majesty and glory of the mountains was equally beautiful. There were grassy hills, rocky peaks and in the distance I could see the snow-caps just above the clouds in the horizon. I realized that just as much as there were people, like me, who love the ocean, there were also a great number of people who love the mountains.

So let's say that the mountains represent our problems. During my season of 40 days, I have already shared some of the big ones on my list. But there were others. There were things that I knew that were wrong for me that I kept around anyway because their beauty attracted me. They were my mountains. I was drawn to their majesty and power and splendor and honestly, those mountains had become a part of my life's landscape. I was used to looking into the distance and seeing them there, so much so that I couldn't imagine life without them. Some were filled with the green, lush grass of low expectations and mediocre standards, while others were made of the rocky terrain of self-doubt and isolation. Others, the truly far peaks that I had not yet even gotten close to, were my bad relationships and negative thoughts. I didn't know a life without mountains.

But I loved my mountains, even though some of them were people who came into my life not because of what they could do for me but what I could do for them. For example, there were certain people who liked how much I put myself down, because it made them feel better about themselves. There were others who knew that they would only have access to me if I remained in this space, so they told me how beautiful my life was, knowing all the while that I needed a change. There were (and this is the hardest to admit) people who I wanted so badly that I cultivated my own helplessness so that they would stay with me and 'rescue' me. I was afraid that if I showed them my vast sea of gifts, talents and character, that they would not want me that way. I would surpass them and be too strong for them. So I hid.

My storm washed away this pretense. It was definitely needed. God knew that. I can't say that I would have wanted Him to wash away all that I had claimed to be and pretended to become, but God does what's right for us even when we don't know that it's right ourselves. Though I did not like the rain at all, I know now that I needed it. I needed it to be where I am today—a climber of mountains, not an observer of them.

In the story of Noah we see that God covered every single mountain "under the entire heaven" with "more than 15 cubits" of rain. God didn't want to leave anything in sight except the ocean. He didn't want to leave anything as a point of reference to what was, but instead reveal the sea of all that could be. If the survivors still saw even the top of a mountain, they would have remembered where they had been and have a reference point for a past that they needed to leave behind. In my life, too, God covered every mountain, so much so that when it was over I saw nothing but possibility. Yes, I was still in the boat and it was still raining, and I had no idea what it was going to be like when everything was over, but I knew it would be nothing like before.

And though the nights were long, as the rain continued to beat down on me, and the days were difficult as I pulled away from all that I considered familiar, I no longer was praying for God to deliver me from my mountains. My prayer now was about my future, because as I looked out into the ocean I knew He had finally and completely erased my past.

## DAY 15

# MIRACLES

*'For I know the plans I have for you,' declares the LORD, 'plans to prosper you and not to harm you, plans to give you hope and a future.' (Jeremiah 29:11 KJV)*

In learning about the miracles of Jesus, I have not found a story yet in which He took time to perform what He promised. Jesus performed more than 30 miracles during this lifetime: healing people, feeding people, casting out demons, walking on water, etc. Every miracle that He performed, as far as the Bible accounts, did not have a delay. Even when Jesus cursed the fig tree, the tree withered immediately.

There have been prayers that I prayed, within my storm season and after it was over, that I did not expect God to answer. Though I was sincere in my prayer and had my heart turned towards him, I didn't think that He would do what I asked. Many times, I have been surprised when I saw the very thing that I asked him for made manifest. This is a testament to my need for more faith. How is it that I can serve a God who can do anything, then limit Him to only what my faith believes to be possible? My prayer and my conduct after I pray should be as though He has already done what I believe He can do. However, this boldness does not come from asking for things for our gain, but when we are walking in the Will of the One who called us.

Once, I was broke and had a high utility bill to pay. I didn't have any idea how I was going to pay it. I prayed to God for a miracle, but my prayer, though sincere, came from my weary body. I had been traveling back and forth to Toronto to spend time with my family and get some badly needed emotional support. I was spent in every sense of the word. To have this bill added on top of everything was more than I could handle. I said a short prayer about it, and then the issue left my thoughts as I prepared for my next trip to see my family.

My family has always been so supportive. The hugs, laughs and food were exactly what my soul needed. They gave me the recharge to go back and face climbing all my mountains. After a weekend well spent, I returned home to a pile of mail. It was late and I put my daughter to bed in her crib before walking downstairs to open it. When I noticed one small envelope in the middle of the pile, I recognized the sender as my life insurance company. I opened the envelope, assuming that they were going to ask for a premium payment or something. As I unfolded the paper I noticed that the bottom piece had a section that was perforated and could be detached. It was a check. As I read the letter it said that they were sending me my portion of the surplus premiums. Because my insurer was a non-profit, they did not keep the profits, but dispersed them as dividends to the policyholders. The money was exactly what I needed to pay my bill!

I sat on my steps and wept. I couldn't believe that God had answered my prayer even though I knew He had the power to. I couldn't believe that this letter had most likely been in my mailbox even before I took my trip, possibly before I found out that I had a bill to pay!!!

I expected that if and when God was going to work a miracle in my life, that it would take time. But God told me that He does not need time to perform His good work in us; it is we who need the time to believe that it is possible. Often, the delay in our deliverance doesn't come from God not being able or ready to answer our prayers, but that we aren't ready for Him to do it. We are not looking, or we have not gone out and opened the doors of opportunity that He has set up for us. When we pray to Him about a situation, we have things to learn that we can only learn in our difficulties, *before* He gives us our miracle.

Many times, I have prayed for days, weeks, months or even years about a need and it seemed like God was not listening. Perhaps, I told myself, I'm not praying hard enough. But when I look back now, I have to admit that I would not be as close to Him now had I not had that time of constant petition then. The length of the trial was not for His benefit, but for mine. I needed to constantly come to the Father and talk with Him, even if it was about the same subject. My biggest growth periods came in the moments that I thought I had to wait for God. It was then that He was able to make me ready for a miracle. He always had it ready. I just needed to be ready to accept it.

# DAY 16

# Over-thinking

*'For my thoughts are not your thoughts, neither are your ways my ways,' declares the LORD... (Isaiah 55:8 KJV)*

My brain is constantly going. The to-do list in my head is always a mile long and items are always being added to it. I am considered dependable by many because I can accomplish a variety of tasks at the same time. Though this trait has helped me many times, it has also been a hindrance.

Prayer is a time when we can shut out the world and focus on the One who created it. My time talking to God is a time I cherish, because He is my best friend. I tell Him everything and I feel His presence surround me when we have our quiet time. This was not always my sentiment regarding prayer, however. During my storm, I would get easily distracted. I would pray and let God know all that was going on, but it felt like I was tasking Him to complete something rather than coming to Him in trust and surrender. My faith was in my ability to do things, and I felt that if He wasn't *doing* what I thought He should, then He wasn't doing things right.

As a result, during my hours of prayer, I would harbor resentment and impatience about what He had not yet done. I would try to speak about His splendor and glory, but I had impatient, even angry questions about why He had not manifested what I needed. Though I knew He had promised an end to my storm, I wanted it over on *my* timeline.

This lack of faith in God's will and my presumptuous faith in my own strength meant that I wouldn't always concentrate or harness the power of prayer. I would come away with some relief, but I was overthinking and not trusting in God's plan.

During this time, I didn't get enough sleep. . My daughter had chronic ear infections and would awaken every two or three hours every night. Between my own stress and my sick child, sleeping through the night became a thing of the past. It wasn't all because my daughter was sick; my mind was constantly going, even after praying, on all that had happened, was happening and needed to happen.

During this time, this passage from Isaiah was God's promise to me. My boat was being tossed like a toy in the storm. I left like I no longer had the foundation of the ground beneath me as the water deepened. But God told me over and over again that what He had in mind for me was better than anything I had thought of for myself.

I didn't expect much for myself during that period. I felt like a failure. To have just turned 30 and have a failed marriage was awful. To be a single mother with little support in a town that I had lived in for 15 years was difficult. To be grappling with loneliness was nearly unendurable. To have to function everyday as though everything was fine because others needed the ministry I was called to provide was agony. These trials tossed my spirit to and fro on the waves of my storm, and in my desperation, I started to think... and think...and overthink.

After a while, the noise in my head became so loud that I couldn't figure out how to pray any more. I felt like the words I was saying were not getting my point across. I knew that God knew everything about me and I was exhausted from trying to figure out my own solutions. Finally, one day, I got down on my knees with my head to the ground and arms stretched in front of me. I knelt there in silence and just tried to be quiet and let God speak to me. It took a while because there was so much noise in my mind, but eventually silence came. I started to surrender to the vision that I had when I prayed: I would imagine Jesus getting off His throne and coming down the steps in His court. I would sit beside Him and He would put His arm around me. Then I would lay my head in His lap. This was a place of pure peace when all my thinking would stop. Envisioning this made me so calm. *I could cry here. I could sleep here. I could rest here.*

Finally, ever so softly, I heard God speak to me. He had always been saying this; my own thoughts and feelings were too loud for me to hear it. He said "I know, and I am here. Trust my thoughts for you." Trust was a huge issue for me (something I'll discuss later) but I did eventually surrender my thinking to Him. I turned it over to Him to sort out, instead of me over-thinking and never finding the solution myself. Life became a lot easier once I got out of my own way and decided to live following His.

# Before the Promise

*After this, the word of the LORD came to Abram in a vision: "Do not be afraid, Abram. I am your shield, your very great reward."*
*But Abram said, "Sovereign LORD, what can you give me since I remain childless and the one who will inherit my estate is Eliezer of Damascus?" And Abram said, "You have given me no children; so a servant in my household will be my heir." Then the word of the LORD came to him: "This man will not be your heir, but a son who is your own flesh and blood will be your heir." He took him outside and said, "Look up at the sky and count the stars—if indeed you can count them." Then he said to him, "So shall your offspring be."*
*(Genesis 15: 1-5 NIV)*

I remember reading this in one of my devotions one morning. I kept reading it over and over again for a few days. God had impressed me not to move from chapters 15-17 until He said so. The story was familiar, one I could recite from memory. God told Abraham that he would have a child. Sarah laughed when she heard the news. Sarah didn't believe and convinced Abraham to take her handmaid Hagar and have a child. He did and there was immediate strife in the home, so much so that eventually Hagar was sent away. It was then that Abraham and Sarah had a son named Isaac.

What was it that God was trying to teach me? It took a while for me to get it, but when he revealed it I couldn't help but cry as I knew He was promising me the same thing.

God's promise to Abraham was that his seed would multiply more than could be counted. Abraham's purpose was to be the father of a great nation. The number of his seed would be more than the stars in the sky and sand on the shores. But when God revealed Abraham's purpose to Him, Abraham had no children. Immediately after this revelation, Abraham asked for a sign that the promise God had just given him would come to pass, but before Abraham could have his sign, God told him he had to make a sacrifice.

God's first lesson to me was that your purpose will always require a sacrifice. In my storm, I remember asking God for many signs. I had been so hurt and bruised by my situation I was scared to trust the voice I was hearing. Especially when it was saying that I would receive the very thing that my heart desired. So I asked God to show me His will and to give me a sign that His will would actually become reality in my life. First, He required me to make a sacrifice. I had to sacrifice my time, my money and my service. I had to be a follower before I could lead. I had to give before I could receive and I had to serve in order to be served.

When you ask God for a sign, don't be surprised if you are required to make a sacrifice first. You may be waiting on God for the promise of healing, but it may require the sacrifice of long suffering. You may be waiting on God for the promise of deliverance, but it will require the sacrifice of patience. You may be waiting on God for the promise of financial blessing, but it will require the sacrifice of self-control. When you ask for a sign, you will be expected to sacrifice something. Your sacrifice is the price you prove to God that you are willing to pay.

After Abraham prepared the sacrifice and lay it on the altar, the Bible says that fowls came down on the carcass and Abraham drove them away. (Gen. 5:11). These birds did not appear out of nowhere. They smelled the sacrifice, saw the sacrifice as he cut it and were planning how to prey on it. The lesson here was crystal clear: *Beware of promise stealers* (Genesis 15:11).

People who have not trusted God with their lives *will* have a problem seeing you trust God with your own. As I moved into my purpose and it was being revealed in my life, the people who I thought would be most supportive were nowhere to be found. Others saw who I was becoming and did not support it. I quickly realized that these people were trying to steal my sacrifice and find out my purpose, and it was much easier to drive them away. I stopped communication with some people, and stopped going to certain places. I was more reserved about sharing my dream and I focused more attention on getting better at my purpose than on seeking validation from others. It was an extremely hard lesson to learn, and it made my lonely days lonelier and my dark nights darker, but God showed me that everything that I had brought with me to this point could not come to where He wanted me to go.

*Psalms 37:32 - The wicked watcheth the righteous, and seeketh to slay him. (KJV)*

There will be people who you call friends who are not your friends; they are waiting to steal your faith. They have smelled promise on you, have seen the purpose in you, and they plan to take your sacrifice from you. They may realize that stealing your sacrifice will not get them any closer to their own God-ordained purpose, but they will not care. The lesson here is simple: *remove these people from your life*. Drive them away.

The Bible says that Abraham had to stand guard over his sacrifice and drive the vultures away. Attacks didn't just come once, but over and over again. He spent blood and sweat to watch his sacrifice and make sure it would fulfill its purpose...so he could fulfill his. Protecting my sacrifice required a lot of effort. I had to guard my heart and my spirit. I had to remind myself that I could do all the things that God had called me to do, and I had to command my spirit to have joy on the many occasions that I was tempted toward sadness and doubt. Protecting your sacrifice will require similar effort.

## DAY 18

# SKIPPED

*When the sun had set and darkness had fallen, a smoking firepot*
*with a blazing torch appeared and passed between the pieces. On that*
*day the LORD made a covenant with Abram and said, "To your de-*
*scendants I give this land, from the Wadi of Egypt to the great river,*
*the Euphrates— the land of the Kenites, Kenizzites, Kadmonites,*
*Hittites, Perizzites, Rephaimes, Amorites, Canaanites, Girgashites*
*and Jebusites."*
*(Genesis 15: 17-21 NIV)*

*When Abram was ninety-nine years old, the LORD appeared to him*
*and said, "I am God Almighty; walk before me faithfully and be*
*blameless. Then I will make my covenant between me and you and*
*will greatly increase your numbers." Abram fell facedown, and God*
*said to him, "As for me, this is my covenant with you: You will be*
*the father of many nations. No longer will you be called Abram; your*
*name will be Abraham, for I have made you a father of many na-*
*tions. I will make you very fruitful; I will make nations of you, and*
*kings will come from you. I will establish my covenant as an everlast-*
*ing covenant between me and you and your descendants after you for*
*the generations to come, to be your God and the God of your descen-*
*dants after you. The whole land of Canaan, where you now reside as*

*a foreigner, I will give as an everlasting possession to you and your*
*descendants after you; and I will be their God."*
*(Genesis 17: 1 -8 NIV)*

God showed me this final lesson in this story and it was so simple: "You need to always be where I am." After Chapter 15 we turn to Chapter 16 and the story of Hagar. Her entire mention in the Bible is housed in this one chapter. For days I read the story of Abraham beginning with Chapter 15 through to Chapter 17. Then one morning, God told me to read it as follows: Genesis 15: 17-21, Genesis 17: 1 -8.

You can read the entire story of Abraham without Chapter 16 and not miss a beat on the manifestation of the promise in his life. Chapter 16 was the fallible human input that caused grief and heartache. Abraham and Sarah decided to "help God" bring the promise in their life to pass, instead of trusting His timing to do what He said He would do all by Himself.

If I tried to describe the many times that I have tried to "help" God, this book would be way too long. I am a strong woman, independent and resourceful. If I need to get something done, I usually do it myself. I feel in my heart that there is nothing I cannot do if I put my mind to it. This, however, does not bode well for a relationship with anyone...especially God. I know that He has given me strength and power to declare and achieve, but I have to constantly remind myself that my job is to do what He says, not to make suggestions to Him about what His plan should be.

And so, jumping ahead of God has cost me some heartache. I've lost money, shed unnecessary tears and had to live with circumstances and outcomes that I put myself in, all because I was trying to make His promise happen my way instead of trusting His way. I recall one time that God had told me I would be moving to the D.C./Maryland/Virginia area, also known as the DMV area. He had given me that message through five different people and I was shocked by it (especially since one of the people was my boss at the time; for a moment I thought I was being fired). But once I let the promise take root in my heart, I thought that I needed to do something. I began to apply for jobs.

I applied for dozens of jobs in the area but I didn't receive any calls or get any interviews. I was totally confused as to why God would give me that message and then not help me achieve it. But the way He wanted the transition and my move to go was much bigger than anything I could have imagined. I was given an assignment in the DMV for more than six months, which allowed me the opportunity to see the area without having to bear the cost of moving. It also gave me the opportunity to work with one of the top agencies in my field, and I was hired into an elite group of people that I would normally not have been exposed to had I tried to get a job on my own.

If Abraham and Sarah had listened and followed God's plan, they would have eliminated Chapter 16 and their lives would have worked out exactly as God had planned. There have also been many decisions that I have made that I wished I hadn't. After jumping the gun with God, so to speak, I would struggle with guilt as the enemy left constant reminders of my mistake, tempting me to wallow in the despair of my actions rather than believe God could still activate His promise. When I saw this lesson, I curled up in my bed in fetal position and wept. I saw that God couldn't be derailed. He could still use me and bring His purpose to pass. Even though I had made so many mistakes in my own Chapter 16, it didn't mean that Chapter 17 wasn't going to happen.

God continued writing my story just as He had planned all along, without any hint of my impatient mistakes – without any hint of my 'chapter 16.' God gave Abraham and Sarah a son, just as He said He would. As the tears flowed that morning, I then realized that God could rewrite my story too. He would not hold my impatience and impertinence against me; the promise of my Chapter 17 was still real and possible. He was waiting for me so that He could skip my mistake and keep writing.

# DAY 19

# SILENCE

*The LORD will fight for you, and you have only to be silent.*
*(Exodus 14:14 ESV)*

Trying to keep the peace during my storm seemed impossible. I did not want to talk to anyone about what I was enduring, but I did want to defend myself when people began throwing accusations. It was evident to everyone around me—those who I once held close and those who were basking in my misfortune—that I was in a storm. My season of rain may have begun without their knowledge, but they were now able to see the evidence of the storm as my spirit began to show signs of wear and tear. I was weeping more at the altar and I pulled back from many people (as there was constant uncertainty about who were my true confidantes).

But the hardest part of all was that many people in my church, leaders and laymen alike, had strong opinions about my situation and made it a point to let me know them. My storm had many different situations, including my divorce, in which the details were private between my daughter's father and myself. Unfortunately there were some people who began to take sides on the issue for a variety of reason, but no matter what the reason was it was a very difficult process to go through.

During the Christmas season, a gentleman from church decided to call me after speaking with my ex-husband. He wanted to give me his opinion of the decisions that we had made and began to berate me on the phone. Because my nerves and emotions were so raw at the time and I was fatigued with my own set of issues and emotions, inviting another one into the mix was more than I could take. This man told me, as he kept poking, that he was being a friend to both of us. I responded by requesting he do exactly what he said "and just be a friend." But he kept pushing, trying to make our situation something that would make him comfortable. I got off the phone as quickly as I could and wept. I was so frustrated and angry. I wanted to call him back and speak all manner of good and bad that was on my mind, but that evening as I was scrolling on Facebook I saw this post from a friend and it jumped out at me:

*The LORD shall fight for you, and ye shall hold your peace. Ex. 14:14 KJV*

I was so tempted to defend myself and my position to this man, but God did not give me the okay to do so. Because I was still talking to Him about all that was within me, I was able to discern when He gave me permission to move in a situation and when not to. And even though, in my mind, I would have been completely justified to let this man know that the business he had just stepped into was in no way near his own, because God had not said yes, I knew that it was not His will at that time.

That was hard.

After all that I had been through, was going through and knew was in my future, to have to hold my peace (even though I was in the right) was a test like none other. I would see this man at church and he wouldn't speak to me. I would have to pray about my spirit to worship, as it would be vexed because of his participation in leading the congregation. I just wanted to scream at him and tell everyone about him. But God told me to be still.

In your season of 40 days and nights, other people will likely be able to see clearly that you are in a storm. Often, they will want to share their opinion as to why you are enduring what you are going through (remember Job's friends?) and what you need to do to "fix" it—whether you want their opinions or not. But speaking out of turn and putting them 'in their place'—even if you are right—before God wants you to do still leaves you in the wrong. I knew that God might have been using my situation as a means to teach this nosy man something, too. I remember praying to God and asking Him why I had to help in someone else's journey when my cross was so hard to bear, but all He kept saying was "Be still."

Well, this man and I, who had a reasonable friendship, did not say anything to each other for two years. I would see him and my spirit would rise up, and we would avoid each other. I did not want to hear another lecture on my divorce. I was obedient to God's Will, and all the Spirit would allow me to do was wave and say "Hello." God did not let me defend myself, but rather forced me to trust that He would fight for me.

Two years later, at the same church, I did a farewell performance. After the service, people came by to wish me well on my move. I gave hugs and took phone numbers with promises to keep in touch. It was such a nice and welcome change to be accepted again in an environment in which I had felt ostracized a couple of years before. At the end of the service this same gentleman came up to me. I saw the remorse in his eyes and all my anger melted as I reached out for my friend once again. He hugged me and said, "I'm sorry for taking sides." Tears welled up in my eyes as the Spirit of healing flowed between us. I was amazed that God had given me the direction and strength to hold my peace and I saw the change in this man as he realized that I had never spoken to him harshly, even though it might have been justified. All God had allowed to flow from me was love, even when I didn't feel it. As a result, this man got to see God's unconditional love, too. He learned that the storm didn't break me and that my season of rain did bring forth fruit.

As I write this, I still breathe a sigh of relief at how God worked that out. I never had to speak my case to anyone, never had to defend myself. God did it all, as he allowed the rain to come down. He still covered me, defended me and fought for me. So to you I say, keep silent. Let God fight for you.

DAY 20

# THE WAITING ROOM

*Wait for the LORD; be strong and take heart and wait for the LORD.*
*(Psalms 27:14 NIV)*

There are more than 100 verses in the Bible that speak about waiting. During my storm, it seemed, as I read, that my devotions often led me to the concept of waiting and my need to learn how to do it more often. I was not a good "waiter." I would stomp and pout at God and complain about all I was going through. I would get frustrated when I didn't see any change and honestly felt like I was not getting what I deserved in my waiting season...and then one day God reminded me of something.

If you ask my mother today, she will tell you that we have always been blessed with amazing doctors. My family lived in a small town called Mottingham when I was a young child and I remember going to see Dr. Masse, who was walking distance from my house. He cared and paid attention to every detail of our health. We never felt rushed when we saw him (though I never liked going to the doctor for fear of the dreaded injection). After we migrated to Canada when I was eight, my mother found a doctor in our neighborhood named Dr. O'Brien. He, too, was an amazing doctor. The care that he gave each patient made you feel like he did not have any other patients except you. You could make an appointment about one particular issue, but while you were with him he gave you the full liberty to talk about anything you needed to. He took time and attention and wrote down little notes to remind himself of key life details. As I got older I was able to go to the doctor on my own, and I still received the same care and attention as I had received when my mother was present.

There was one time we visited the office because my little brother was sick. My mother was home alone with us and packed up my middle brother and me and drove us all down to the office. We didn't have an appointment, but she felt that the severity of my baby brother's condition was such that he needed to see the doctor as soon as possible. The attendant put our names on the list and we waited to be called. Because Dr. O'Brien was so good, it was common to have long, long waits. However, hardly anyone ever left. People were willing to wait for him because they knew the care they were going to receive would be exactly what they needed. So we waited.

And waited. And waited.

For almost four hours we waited as my mom paced up and down with my brother trying to bring him some comfort. Finally she asked the receptionist what the holdup was, only to find out that the doctor had been called away to the hospital on an emergency but was on his way back. A few minutes later we were called into his office. When we got in his office, my mother got straight down to business, knowing that the care she was about to receive was worth the wait she had endured.

My storm felt like one long wait. I wished over and over again that it would just be over, but it kept going. God never changed His timing just because I was in the waiting room. He actually left me in the waiting room a bit longer each time I complained about how long I had been in there. Because as much as I needed to receive when I saw Him, there was also something else that I could only learn *in* the waiting room. Until I learned the lesson in the waiting room, I would not have the capacity to receive all that was waiting for me with God.

He told me not to leave the waiting room. Many times I was tempted to forget the commitment I had from Him that my breakthrough was coming and just do what I pleased. Many times I was tempted to give up believing that a change would happen. Even though I knew that my very presence in the waiting room meant that I had a problem that I needed help with, when the wait got too long, there were moments that I wrestled with the idea of just living with my condition.

The hardest thing about waiting for my doctor was focusing on waiting for my doctor. The medical office provided reading material, had art on the walls and often my mother would bring toys and games for us to play with. Sometimes we would make new friends with other people who were also waiting. Whenever I focused on those things, the wait didn't seem as bad. I actually learned some things from the reading. I was able to take time to appreciate the art on the walls and I made great memories playing with my brothers and the other children. While I was waiting in my storm, it was always easier when I focused on reading God's word. Studying and recalling His promises calmed my nerves tremendously. I also took time to appreciate all the good things and beauty that I did have. For all that I was waiting on God for, I would always have to admit that He had already done so much for me in my life that it was too much to name. When I turned my attention to these things in the "waiting" season, I found myself praising as I waited. My solemn steps moved quicker with joy, and I had peace in my heart that when He was ready to "see" my situation He would handle it just as He had done for me so many times before.

My waiting season also provided fellowship with others. I came to know people I already knew better, and was introduced to fellow believers. We exchanged encouragement and helped each other through. I was blessed with people who rejoiced in my blessings with me, which made them feel even greater, and who mourned my losses alongside me, which helped lighten the load. I would not have made many of the friendships that I have today if my appointment had called without a time of waiting.

When my appointment finally came, God did exactly what I believed He could do, and the wait made the receipt of His deliverance so much better.

**Special Video Message -**
**Watch #ThePrayerOfAnInsecureWoman**

www.LydiaElle.com/booklinks

# DAY 21

# THE RAIN CAME

*And after the seven days the floodwaters came on the earth.*
*(Genesis 7:10 NIV)*

I looked around me and couldn't believe where I was. Everything was boarded up and covered. There were no wires, no cables, no bars on the bed, and the lights shone an ugly mustard yellow color on the pale green walls. Nothing about this was inviting at all. The bed was reasonably soft, though it was clearly not made for comfort, and there was no pillow. I was trying to be present in the moment as best I could, but it all seemed so surreal. Every word I said left my mouth as if with an echo, as though being recorded by "me" watching the whole experience from the outside. I felt like I was having an out-of-body experience. I continued the internal conversation with myself:

> "I think I'm okay. But I'm so, so tired. No one can ever find out about this. I just want to sleep and never wake up..."

Then the nurse came in. My angel-friend who had brought me let go of my hand and said, "Okay honey, they need to check some things. Can you sit up for a second?" I thought I was moving and alert, but as I looked at the faces of those in the room with me I could see that what I thought was vibrant energy was really worrisome lethargy.

Earlier that day I had conducted business as usual. I got up, showered and went to pump milk for my baby girl. She was eight months at the time and had a raging appetite. Once that was satisfied, I nursed her and kissed her softly before I gave her to my brother and his wife, who were helping me with her at the time. Then I got dressed and headed off to work. I had an oatmeal smoothie in the car and took my pill. For the last four months I had been seeing a counselor and had been diagnosed with depression. It wasn't something you could really see on me, because I dressed reasonably well and could still function. But concentration was difficult for me. I was stressed beyond belief and had no down time as the financial welfare of my family lay squarely on my shoulders. I was also the general contractor for my house that had flooded eight months earlier and two days earlier, I had been told by my insurance that they would no longer pay for the apartment that we were living in. So despite the fact that my house was not yet habitable, I had to move out of my apartment. So that day, as I drove to work, I found myself with the very real possibility of being homeless.

But I was sure I was okay. Yes, I had cried a lot and had no clue how this was going to work out, but I thought I was okay. The day I found out about the apartment I came home from work and nursed my daughter. As I sat on the coach talking to my brother and sister-in-law, I burst into uncontrollable tears. I just couldn't stop crying; the despair within me was so deep, concentrated and final. My brother tried everything to console me, but nothing worked, nor could I articulate what was wrong with me except to say, "I'm so tired."

So there I was, looking around at this pale room with nothing in it. No warmth, no love, no comfort. I believe my friend did the best thing by bringing me to the hospital, though I would never have thought that I needed it. I didn't have a cut or a bruise. Nothing hurt or was sore. But I ached in a place that no doctor could see because the pain was in the depths of my soul...and I was so, so tired.

*The LORD is nigh unto them that are of a broken heart; and saveth such as be of a contrite spirit. (Psalm 31:18 KJV)*

To think that God was with me in that moment still brings me to tears. The spirit of depression had been on me for months and no matter how many pills, songs, prayers, and scriptures I tried, I just couldn't shake it. At around 11 o'clock that morning, I called my doctor and the nurse practitioner got on the phone. I was calling to ask for a higher dose of anti-depressants, and she asked me why. I couldn't really articulate the pain I was feeling and just started to cry. All I said was, "I need more pills, please, please, I need more pills." She feared that I was in a very bad place, which I definitely was, and had fleeting thoughts of taking my own life. What had kept me going to that point was the fact that I had a little person who depended on me for everything. Though I felt that my life was a complete disaster, I didn't want to leave her alone. It was my love for her that saved me, for in those dark moments when I didn't have enough love for myself to want to be here, I stayed for her.

That day I was diagnosed with situational depression and was not released from it until I got out of a very bad place. I made it to the hospital that day only by the grace of God.

If there was a time that began my season of 40 days of rain, this would be it. Though my depression had been going on for months, this felt like the beginning of a tempest. I was awakened to a heavy burden, and though I knew that God would lift it, I had to wait until He chose to do it. I am not saying He left me in depression, but the circumstances that I faced did not change overnight. There were relationships that needed healing, relationships that needed ending, decisions to be made, and steps that needed to be taken. There was a lot of work that I had to do, and the first was to believe that I deserved better.

I share this story for a few reasons. The first is to bring awareness to depression, which is a very real, serious illness that many people suffer with.

It is not one that is spoken about often due to the stigma of mental illness, the misunderstanding that depression is just "feeling sad", and the difficulty that people have in trying to help someone with it. Within the body of Christ we have many who are sick and suffering, including those of a broken heart, who need our love and care as we pray and support their healing.

I also share the story of my pain because I recall God's presence even in the midst of my suffering. I didn't really speak to Him, and when I tried I didn't know what to say, but my thoughts were still directed towards Him, even in my confusion. I believe that this was still prayer. So often we think that prayer has to have a particular look, feel and flavor, but prayer is nothing more than constant, heartfelt, humble communication with the Great "I Am." Because I was so brokenhearted, I know that my feeling that God was near was not something I imagined, but rather what actually happened. No matter how alone I felt, He was close at hand, feeling all the pain I endured and helping me through it.

Even without words, you can still speak to Him. You can still reach Him. Know that He is so close that He has heard your thoughts...even in the rain, He has not left you. It is during this time that He is closest.

# DAY 22

# MARATHON

*Therefore, since we are surrounded by such a great cloud of witnesses,*
*let us throw off everything that hinders and the sin that so easily*
*entangles. And let us run with perseverance the race marked out for*
*us. (Hebrews 12:1 NIV)*

I'm not much of a runner. I used to detest cross country when I was in elementary school because I would, after only a few laps, feel like my lungs were going to fall out of my chest and flop down the hill.

As I got older and I made the commitment to take care of my body—both for my health and to improve upon the gift of singing which God had given me—I tried to adopt running as part of my workout. Over time it got easier and I even came to enjoy some moments of solitude, as I could talk to God and pray while I worked to improve my stamina.

During one cold winter night early in my storm, God (as He often did) woke me up to talk. The door to my bathroom was slightly ajar, allowing a few rays of light to fall through. As God and I conversed, I lay on my pillow, staring at the ceiling. I was tired, because my daughter's cold had ruined her sleep and, thus, my own. But as thoughts flooded my mind about running, God began to teach me this lesson.

A marathon course is 26.3 miles long. It is not something that most people can just decide to do today and execute tomorrow. It takes training, discipline and will to begin, endure and finish the race.

When a runner begins to train for a race, they can begin by running shorter distances. Some join a team of runners who are also training for an upcoming race. As a team they become connected and encourage each other as they train. They help improve each other's strides, breathing and technique, unearthing each other's strengths as well as weaknesses. But the end goal, when race day comes, is that everyone will cross the finish line.

Another key aspect to preparing for the race is the practical training. Most marathon courses are not level, so just training in a gym on a treadmill won't prepare a runner for all the conditions he or she will face. Runners must practice in rough terrain, train for the uphill sections and the steep downhill stretches. They must train in different weather conditions and temperatures, because it may not be sunny on race day. They must train in as many different environments as possible in order to minimize the chance of a surprise on race day.

Finally, runners must take care of their bodies. This doesn't just mean exercise and diet. The mind must be trained to endure and the emotions must be controlled, so that when the body wants to quit the mind can overrule it. Each day that runners train, they must push a little further and climb a little higher, telling themselves that they can push past their suffering and finish the course no matter how they feel.

When race day comes you can hear the cheers of joy and motivation as the runner who worked so hard to prepare is finally at the starting line. Looking around, you can recognize the optimism each participant has. Each believes that everything is possible—because it is.

Around the halfway mark, things begin to change. Though the runner has run this distance before, this mile marker feels different. The reason is because around that halfway mark, the runner becomes aware of conflict. With all the training, there was no training that could prepare the runner for unexpected conflict. At the same time, without the training the conflict would completely derail the runner and his or her goals would be lost.

The first conflict a runner faces is other runners. Those who he trained with as a team have become rivals. They still want the runner to cross the finish line, but they don't want him or her to cross *before they do*. Because the runner has trained with them, they are able to speak negatively in ways that they know will penetrate the heart and sap the will. They will dig up old insecurities and fears in an attempt to get him to quit. It is here that the runner must keep going until he is at the finish line.

The second conflict is internal. Some of the negative seeds that other competitors plant in his spirit will take root and grow. His own self-doubts will flower as well. At this point, the runner must dig deep within himself and use all his will to remember who he is. He must tell himself that the goal he set out to achieve is still within his grasp. Despite the pain of betrayal and gossip, cliques and isolation, and rejection and exclusion, he must keep faith in himself, his training and his determination. He must and will believe in himself and his ability to make it to the finish line.

When the runner has passed through the first two conflicts and sees the finish line approaching, one final conflict will present itself. His body will want to give up. The pain will be so excruciating that he will believe that he cannot survive. It will be as though his body is telling him that he cannot do what he set out to do. It is here, in the darkest moment, that it is most important to continue to put one foot in front of the other. It is now a matter of just one more step, and then another. Not even the thought of all the distance covered will help at this point, because the body will be so fatigued and in so much pain that nothing but rest will bring any comfort. But this is when the discipline of mind over body will matter most. It is here that the will must be strongest above all else. Even if others pass you in the race stay encouraged and know that all you have to do is cross the finish line. Though you may see other people running, each has their own race with their own challenges and goals. Don't be distracted by them, because your race was created just for you and you have everything you need to finish it. Stay in the race, and I know that you will.

## DAY 23

# I HAD TO SING...

*I will sing to the LORD as long as I live. I will praise my God to my last breath! (Psalms 104:33 NLT)*

It was supposed to be a trio. Well, not really a trio, but each of us was supposed to sing one of the solos for the medley the director had chosen. Our residential college choir was doing one of their reunion concerts and the director called upon me to sing a lead for one of the songs. I was hesitant because I was at the height of my storm. At this point, it was more than one storm; it was the colliding of several. There were many issues I was trying to work through on a personal level. I didn't really want to sing at all because I felt like everything I was dealing with was written on my forehead for the world to see.

The truth is, they probably didn't see as much as I thought they did, because they were dealing with their own messes. This was a ploy of the enemy to keep me wallowing in such self-doubt and pity that I crippled myself with my fear of being judged. So when the choir director called, my first response was no. I knew that I wouldn't be able to hold it together, given the songs he had selected. However, he promised me that I would not be up singing these songs by myself. I would be part of a trio. Encouraged by the idea that I would not be alone and would have support in case I succumbed to my emotions, I said yes.

Rehearsal day came, and I went to the youth center of the local church where the concert was to be held. I entered the room as I usually did, hoping that no one would notice, but the expressions of excitement and encouragement that greeted me made that impossible. Still, the director and the members of the choir and band welcomed me warmly. This was not my first time singing in front of these people, but it was my first time coming forward during this season of my life. Soon the rehearsal turned to my song selection and I got up. Then I noticed that the people the director had said would be singing with me did not move. I turned and made eye contact with him, realizing that the conversation we were having with our eyes would be all that I could have. I had to prepare to sing all three songs. And the songs, at this moment, were my heart's cry:

"Secret Place"
"Under His Wings"
"In His Safety"

There could not be a better combination of music to sum up all that I desired of God. I was in need of a place to hide and be in secret for a while so I could recover from the blows life had recently dealt me. I longed to know I was under His wings, being sheltered from any further hurt and pain. I needed to know that my heart was safe, even for a little while, so it could be healed without any further blows. But as much as I needed to speak to God about all of those things, I did not relish the idea that I would be doing so in the company of more than a thousand people! I wanted to back out, but I knew that God had called me to do this at this time, in this state of mind. As much as I hated the idea of being so vulnerable, I would do anything for Him. Since He gave me this gift, He could use it as He pleased...even if I didn't always agree.

And so I had to sing. I went into my mental space of preparation and conversation with the Father as the concert began and led up to my performance. People around me came to talk and greet me, but I wanted to stay centered and focused. I had no idea what was about to happen, but I knew that something was.

Finally, the choir assistant called for me. I was directed to stand stage left and took that moment to pray by myself beside the wall. I faced it and cried out to God to give me another way. I knew that my heart was heavy, which means that He knew it was too. I knew that I was broken, which means that He knew too. I wanted Him to either give me healing so that I could sing on the other side of this storm or a way out so I didn't have to. He said no.

I walked up on stage and took the microphone. Because I wasn't going to be part of a trio after all, I'd had to learn one of the songs, written by a choir member, just that evening and was quite nervous about it. However, once the music started God took over.

*This world sometimes seems cruel and cold...*

For only the first two words, I remember being technical about my vocals. By the time I got to the second line, though a thousand plus people were present and even more were watching from home on the Internet, it became a conversation between my Father and me.

I made it through the first song without too much emotion, though the tears were welling up inside of me the entire time and I felt so exposed that I let my hair cover more of my face than usual. By the time we got to the second song, I felt the emotion start to beckon to be released. Then the third song started...

*I'm in His safety...*

I knew at this moment that I was not only exposed, but probably would be overly so by the end of the song. I realized that was exactly where God wanted me to be. I knew that as much as I was fighting to stay closed off, He wanted me to be open. The air of His presence on the wounds of my soul did sting at first...but by the middle of the song I felt better. It wasn't because my wounds were healed, but because I had now released them. My vulnerability was so blatant in this song that my only refuge was to turn around and face the choir. Even doing that, though, I had to lift my hands to God and surrender myself to Him.

After the performance was over I gave the mic back to the director, who continued the appeal that I had started. I walked off the stage, picked up my purse at the bottom of the steps and walked out the side exit. My cousin met me outside and prayed with me. He knew the heaviness I was feeling and helped me carry it. After we prayed I got in my car and drove home. I didn't even know if the concert was over. And I didn't care. I didn't want to talk to anyone about it. I needed the silence of God because I had just been so loud about Him. That night changed me. Nothing major happened to change my situation, and some pain actually got worse, but the experience changed me because I realized what God had placed in me would always have to come out. He gave me a voice as a gift and I had to sing.

**Watch the performance behind this story:
'Secret Place LIVE - During the storm'**

www.LydiaElle.com/booklinks

## DAY 24

# 1,2,3 SLEEPING

*When you lie down, you will not be afraid; when you lie down, your sleep will be sweet. (Proverbs 3:24)*

When my daughter was younger, we would play a game that was supposed to help her go to sleep. The game never achieved its purpose, but it was always fun to play pretend with her anyway. It was called "1, 2, 3 Sleeping" and it called for one of us to count and then say, "sleeping." The other person was supposed to fall asleep. Like I said, it never really worked but she thought it was the funniest thing ever. At any time and place I could say, "One, two, three, sleeping!" and she would know exactly what to do.

During my time in the South one of the things I had to get used to was tornado season. My first tornado shook me completely and made me question why I had decided to attend Oakwood University in the first place. However, over time I found that the tornado warnings and alarms were really a precautionary measure; rarely did anything more damaging than rain come down from the heavens. So in April of 2011, when I heard on the news that a tornado was expected, I didn't think much of it. Having been through so many warnings, I paid no attention. My cousin was in town and needed a ride to see a friend of his. I told him that I could take him, but would first have to pick up my daughter from daycare. As we drove down the street (everything in Huntsville, Alabama, is fairly close so it was literally down the street) I noticed that the clouds had begun to change. Their color was one I had never seen, and I figured I might need to brace for a storm that was little more intense than I was used to.

As I dropped my cousin off, the rain began, and it went from a sprinkle to buckets very quickly. I rushed home and got my baby inside. She was just beyond one year old then so I made her some dinner and then got her ready for bed. Now for all the years that I had lived in Huntsville, I knew the things to do to prepare for a tornado, including where to take shelter. However, that night I was so tired that my prayer to God was simple.

"Tonight, Lord, I just want to sleep. If you decide that I should die then no amount of preparing can stop it, and if you decide that I should remain alive then no tornado can stop it."

I tucked my daughter snugly beside me, with the thought that if anything did happen then at least she would be beside me and I wouldn't have to wade through debris to find her. We went upstairs to sleep in my bed. I do not remember tossing or turning at all.

The next morning, I woke to devastation. The power was out citywide and the tornado had missed my neighborhood by only a few miles. I smiled when I thought about what God had done for me. It was not because of any elaborate prayer (I didn't even pray aloud), but it was because I resolved that God was in control of all things.

As I thought back to that situation later on in my storm I remember God saying to me, "Remember how you acted during the tornado? Completely carefree and in full faith that my Will would be done no matter what happened around you?" I replied "Yes, God."

"You should act that way all the time. It will save you a world of stress."
I was silent. He was right. That night I took on absolutely no stress about my
situation or the doom that seemed to loom over my city. I just trusted that
God would do what He wanted and went to sleep.

One, two, three, sleeping....

# DAY 25

# THE EYE

*"The LORD has established Zion, and in her his afflicted people will find refuge." (Isaiah 14:32 NIV)*

I was so snug in my bed it was a miracle that my girlfriend was able to convince me to get out. Earlier that week she had told me about a concert at her church featuring a singer with a voice that I absolutely loved, and I had promised her that I would come and support. Paul has to be one of the greatest tenors of all time, not just for his melodic voice and indescribable control, but because he has the unique ability to take you exactly where He is and then show you Jesus! I had known him and sung with him for years, so I knew how much of a treat a full concert of his would be, but I lived almost an hour away...and did I mention I was snug in my bed?

But my friend convinced me to get out. I knew I needed to be in the presence of the King and this concert would do just that. Every time I had sung with Paul, I had left with less hurt than I arrived with. His voice has a healing quality and because I was in such turmoil, dealing with the effects of the stormy time in my life, I knew that I needed to be there that night.

So I got up and got dressed. The spirit tugged on my heart as I put my jeans on. Not because I see a problem with wearing jeans to church, but because there was the quick nudge that I might be up front and needed to dress appropriately. In silent rebellion, however, I continued to pull up my jeans and put on a summer top, then cover it with a small sweater. I liked to be cozy and as I visualized myself snug in the back of the congregation taking in the music and focusing on God, I was sold that this outfit was perfect for the evening.

I drove the almost hour distance from Arlington to Baltimore and got to the church just as they were finishing praise and worship. My friend was ushering so I sat on the side so that she could see me. It was just a temporary location to get her attention, but just as I sat down Paul walked in. He saw me and greeted me warmly. I was happy to see him too, as the genuine care and love for Jesus twinkled in his eyes. His presence allowed my spirit to breathe a sigh of relief; it felt comfortable showing the cracks and broken places that I hid from those who didn't know me. He couldn't talk for long but he said, "I'm glad you're here. Stay close."

I quickly realized that he may have been planning to call me up to sing. In rebellion again, I went and sat in the back...where I had planned to sit all along.

The concert began and was just as I had imagined it. From the first note I was taken up, covered in Jesus, and felt some of the pain leaving. I was in total thanks to God for the moment, as I didn't often have the chance to be in church and not lead. I relished every moment.

My sweater was a bright yellow, and midway through the concert I took it off. The air conditioning was not on high as I had expected, and as the night progressed the room got a little warmer. As we approached what I thought was the end of the concert, I noticed the ushers getting into place. I breathed a sigh of relief as I realized this was the offering. The pastor came up and solicited the congregation to give out of support for Paul and to help the local cause the concert had been set up for. Right after this, Paul got back up and began to introduce the next half of his program. But he was squinting around the room as if he either couldn't see or was looking for someone. I swallowed hard, trying to dismiss the idea that he was looking for me. Finally, he said my name.

"Lydia."

If there is one thing that God has corrected within me, it is my spirit of submission. I was never fond of the idea during my teen years, but as I grew older and studied the word for myself, I asked God to show me how to be a woman and how to treat a man. He showed me that in the presence of a man, I should not be in combat with him in word, deed or in spirit, but should submit to his authority in the Lord.

So when Paul called me, I was not going to leave him hanging. First, because he was a man of God; second, because he was my friend. I hurried to put my sweater back on, and thought of my rebellion with God as I had gotten dressed a couple of hours earlier. God knew that I would be called upon, and I should have heeded his prompting and dressed better. Not because I needed to look a certain way, but so that I could be comfortable as I did what He created me to.

I took the stage bewildered. Paul and I didn't practice anything, nor did we discuss any format. He told the congregation about me being his sister as I stood clueless as to what was going to come next. I didn't really hear the words that he said, because I was having a conversation with God about what I needed to do, but as his speech came to a close, I realized it was my time. Paul's final words to the crowd were, "Lydia will now come to you in her own way."

That was it. He didn't pick a song for me. He just told me to present myself to them. It was funny to me that Paul had an idea of what "my way" was, but I had no clue. I was still wrestling with so many issues, fighting off so many demons and waging so many battles, that I couldn't even see the way, let alone recognize what was mine.

So I talked. I already felt that every one of the hundreds of eyes there could see my pain. So I told the people that God does things in His own way and in His own time. I told them that in that moment I was in the worst tornado of my life. And then it came to me, as God reminded me that I knew of tornadoes.

A tornado is one of nature's most deadly forces. It can level cities in a matter of minutes, leaving a trail of havoc and mayhem as it goes. But one thing about tornadoes that I find interesting is that they all have an eye. The eye of the tornado is the center and in this spot you do not feel its destructive winds. All manner of craziness may be going on around you, but in the eye of the tornado it is peaceful.

As I stood there and explained what God taught me about tornadoes, he prompted me to tell them that as tumultuous as my life was, and as crazy as everything around me had been, God had kept me at peace in the eye of the tornado. As I was telling them this, I realized He was telling me! As much as I wanted to have a private moment of praise I knew that there were others in the congregation who not only felt what I was saying but needed to know that they could make it through their storms, too. As I settled in with the thought that God was giving me peace, I sang a familiar song near and dear to my heart:

"Beams of Heaven as I go..."

DAY 26

# TRUST AND OBEY

*While he lived on earth, anticipating death, Jesus cried out in pain*
*and wept in sorrow as he offered up priestly prayers to God.  Because*
*he honored God, God answered him.  Though he was God's Son,*
*he learned trusting-obedience by what he suffered, just as we do.*
*(Hebrews 5:7-8 MSG)*

"When we walk with the Lord in the light of His Word,
What a glory He sheds on our way!
While we do His good will, He abides with us still,
And with all who will trust and obey.

Trust and obey, for there's no other way
To be happy in Jesus, but to trust and obey."

Though God was in the entire process of my storm, some days were more difficult
than others. Most of my rough days came about because I brought things on
myself.  It was not so much the circumstances that made the days difficult, but in
attempting to make the storm easier I was not always following His instructions.

A friend once told me something that I needed to hear.  I didn't want
to hear it at the time, but it was necessary for me to move forward in my

development. A part of my resistance to his counsel was the fact that he had been the source of some pain in my life. If I stayed in the space of remembering the hurt, that would relieve me from having to heed his counsel, no matter how wise it was. But what he was saying—that all the pain I was experiencing not entirely his fault—was the truth. I didn't listen to the voice within me that tried to warn and guide me. I trusted God on the back end of my experiences instead of obeying Him through them.

And that was where I was: on the back of a grueling emotional experience that I had made even more difficult. The words from the hymn writer, John H. Sammis, bring together two concepts that I had often brushed over as synonymous. "Trust and obey" were words that to me meant the same thing, but while they are two sides of the same coin, their meanings are different. To trust means that I believe God will bring me through whatever I am currently dealing with. To obey means to listen to His instruction as I am going through it.

Even Jesus, when He was here on earth, had to learn "trusted-obedience." He needed not only to trust God to keep him going as he cried out for deliverance, but to follow his instructions even if it meant he would not be delivered. This is an amazing lesson that God gave me as I was showering to prepare for a praise team rehearsal. He asked me plain and simply, "Lydia, what if I do not deliver you? Would you still trust me? Would you still obey?"

I wanted to stand as the great believer I was striving to be, but I knew in my heart that I could not say yes. This showed me that I trusted God's hand based on what He was giving me, rather than His total will for my life. And because I didn't trust His will, I didn't always obey it. I was at a crossroads. God chose the path that I was on, but I didn't have to experience all the potholes. If I had obeyed Him without question, I would have heard His guidance and listened as He instructed me on what to avoid. My disobedience caused heartache, sleepless nights, tears, self-doubt, and a delay in the development of my relationship with God. The grief I experienced was blinding me from moving to another dimension with Him.

To tell the truth, I considered myself to be like Job. I felt that the trials and troubles that I was going through were to test me, and that God wanted to show me off because He knew that I would be faithful to Him despite everything. I thought that the things that were happening to me were due to no fault of my own. This was a very comforting thought that made my circumstances easier to handle. In taking none of the blame for my current situation, I lacked the perspective that I needed to change it. Nor did I realize that my own disobedience was a part of the journey too.

But I wasn't like Job. I was much more like David with Bathsheba. Having been told by my friend that everything was not someone else's fault, I had felt the anger of indictment and denial, so I went to God and prayed. I realized that I bore much of the blame for all that I was feeling. Yes, I had trusted in God to deliver me, but I had often taken advantage of His grace with my own misconduct.

As I read the verse, I thought, "Who am I?" If Jesus, who was perfect, had to learn this lesson, how much more so did I need to? I needed to trust *and* obey. I needed to head the counsel of my friend *and* I needed to let God continue His work of perfecting these principles while in my storm. Only then would I really see what I was made of, what my faith was made of, what my trust was made of and what my obedience was made of.

DAY 27

# THE YES MAN

*But now thus says the LORD, he who created you, O Jacob, he who
formed you, O Israel: "Fear not, for I have redeemed you; I have
called you by name, you are mine."
(Isaiah 43:1 KJV)*

As my storm season was coming to an end God was able to purge a very bad
habit within me. Due to various situations and events of my past, I had a
deep rooted doubt about myself. It wasn't that I didn't know what I could do
or was unclear of my abilities, but I was also looking for validation of those
gifts. Prior to my storm, I would do my best to bolster my confidence when I
made a decision, and for the most part I would look like I was sure, but I was
always silently looking for approval and validation.

Even when I got it I can't say that it made me any surer of myself.
Sometimes, it just barely appeased my need, which would cause me to go in
search of more validation. No, the solicitation was not outright or obvious,
but my hesitation in doing God's will was clearly evident in my trail of unfin-
ished plans and second guesses.

My problem was that I was confusing validation with confirmation.
Every time I got a message from God I was so unsure of myself that I questioned if what I heard was really true...especially when it came to my dreams.

Then in devotion one day God told me that He was the One who created me and He was the One who had called me for my purpose. Why was I constantly seeking other people to define what I was supposed to do and be? Who knew me no better than I knew myself? It made total sense! I was looking for a "yes man" instead of looking for the answer from God.

My storm season broke this habit in me. As God took people out of my life, my dependence on Him grew exponentially and He became my first and only Source for the answers and approval I needed.

Who better to go to with my dreams and ideas but the One who created me to come up with them? If God made me and called me, then He would know best what I was dreaming of—and He would make it possible. I didn't need to hear a 'yes' from anyone except Him. It was only after I fortified my confidence in His approval that I saw doors open that had been shut for so long. My dependence on Him to make a way proved to be the best way! If others said no to anything I was doing, I could move forward boldly and confidently once I had a "yes" from He who was most important.

Did I need the storm to figure this out? Maybe not, but I can say that I am not sure I would have surrendered my need for validation in any other way.

# Don't Ask, Don't Tell

*And thine ears shall hear a word behind thee, saying, This is the way, walk ye in it, when ye turn to the right hand, and when ye turn to the left. (Isaiah 30:21 KJV)*

There was a conversation that I had with God almost from the first day of my storm. I felt a small nudge within me, especially when one of my best friends told me that he was going to study the ministry. I thought he was absolutely crazy! Not because there is anything wrong with studying the ministry, but because we had both been math majors together. He had gone into a career that was well-matched for those skills and so had I. So when I got a call out of the blue that he was going to go back to school to get a masters in pastoral services, I was a little taken aback.

We would have long conversations about the Word, and his perspective was always so refreshing. It wasn't because he was giving me some deep theological perspective grounded in the doctrines and beliefs that we had both held to all our lives. Rather it was because he was all right with me asking questions that challenged them. I felt safe speaking with him in this manner because he knew that I just needed to know for myself. He would tell me all the time that when he got a church, he would love for me to come and be his associate pastor, and I would grimace every time. During this time I was the financial chair for my church and I helped with that area only. The position did require me to speak very briefly on occasion, but I took each moment that I stood before the people of God so seriously that I began to have more frequent conversations with the Father about taking a greater role in ministry.

In these conversations, I would always say, "God there is no way that you want me to go back to school. It just doesn't make any sense. Considering all the financial obligations that I currently have, where would I find the money to complete yet another degree… and where on earth would I find the time?" I already had three degrees; pursuing another made no sense.

However, the first time I did the intro for the offertory, I broke down. It was a weighted moment as I realized that my congregation was actually getting a message in my words *despite* my setbacks. I cried when I went back to my seat, and after the service was over there were a number of people who told me that I should be a pastor. My reply: "Uh…no!"

Yet each time I had to speak to the congregation, I was more convicted in my delivery. It felt as though God was giving me a lesson to share the night before I had to present. By the third time that I spoke in front of the church, many people, including our head elder and a dear sister, began to call me Pastor Lydia. By this point, the conversation between God and I on the subject was loud and frequent. Yes, I had a conviction to serve God. Yes, I knew there were special messages that He had given me for His people. Yes, I needed to make sure that I delivered them on His behalf. But I still didn't think that it would require my becoming a pastor.

Finally, I decided to just ask God the question. I didn't really want to, because I was afraid of the answer, but I needed confirmation and He was my source for all things. I had been attending a smaller church close to my house by this time (almost a year into my storm) and as I walked into the church I asked God a simple question: "God, if you want me to study the ministry then let someone tell me that today." As I arrived at the church they were having lesson study (my favorite part of the service). On this day, it was a church-wide study in which everyone would study together instead of breaking into smaller groups. I do not remember what the question was, but I recall my response:

> "God is not something like a genie that we rub and make our three requests, with Him obligated to fulfill them. He is not something to be checked off as a weekly or even daily ritual so that we can say that we have clocked sufficient time with Him. Speaking with Him is not something that we do for His benefit, but a daily, hourly, moment by moment state of being that over time refashions our hearts and minds. If we are doing all of this merely to fulfill an obligation, then we have already missed fulfilling it. Because the obligation is the relationship, not the ritual."

The church was silent when I finished. The pastor who was leading the lessons joked and said that he could just do the altar call now. I went back to my seat and sat, knowing that I had said something that helped someone else, but not realizing the impact that that moment would have on the rest of my life. A gentleman, just after the break, came up to me afterwards and said, "I need to speak to the lady who just spoke so eloquently in class." We chatted briefly about my having learned those lessons the hard way, and all the while I was hearing him speak my nerves were on edge; I thought he was the one who God was going to use to let me know that I needed to go to school. But we finished our chat and then he went back to his seat.

My daughter was visiting her father, so my plan was to go home and get some much-needed rest. I was making a dash for my car and didn't stop to talk to anyone. I was hoping that no one would speak to me and I would not have to go to school, since God did not send the sign. But just as I was about to walk out the door, a sister (the same one from my other church) stopped me in the hallway and said, "Girl you know you need to be a pastor!"

I cannot say that I was jumping for joy when she said that. But I had peace that I had finally gotten an answer. I had asked the question that I didn't want to ask and got the answer I was hoping I would not get. But I had known, deep down, what His answer would be. I enrolled in school that week.

# DAY 29

# SAYING AND DOING

*God is love. (1 John 4:8 KJV)*

I thought that love would fix everything. I thought that if I had someone who would accept me for all that I was and was not, I would have what I needed to make it through my storm. I never made this known out loud, but every day my heart was hurting as I didn't feel that anyone really loved me. I often felt alone, and because of the pain of previous experiences I shut myself away from any real human connection in fear that the agony I had once lived would make another cameo appearance in my life.

I knew that God's love was supposed to be enough; I wanted it to be. I prayed honestly with Him about my situation. "Jesus, I love you and know that you are going to be with me through all of this, but I need a hug today.'" My need for something as simple as a hug could consume me for days—even weeks—if my daughter was away visiting her father. I could go for over a week without any human physical contact and I didn't know how I would make it. I was starved for affection and connection.

Often I would come home from work, get in my bed and cry. Cry because I was so lonely, because the loneliness was bitter to the point of poisoning my belief that the storm would pass. Cry because I didn't see how things were going to change. I would cry as I thought of all the people who had promised me love at one time or another who had decided not to love me anymore.

I realized after a time that each person who had promised me love did the best they could. It may not have been all that I had imagined it to be, but what I was imagining was a perfect love. And how could I expect a perfect love from an imperfect person? There was no such thing.

My expectations of the people in my life were often too lofty. It was not their fault, but mine, that I had experienced so much disappointment. Sure, some behavior may have been intentionally hurtful, and some people had acted in blatant disregard for my feelings. (I do not excuse anyone who plays with the heart of another). Despite all of that, I should have known that I could only find my perfect love in the One who is perfect and put the rest of my love experiences in the proper context.

What God did during my storm was so beautiful that I cried the day I realized it. He *is* love. He is the perfect love I was looking for all my life and He sends me love in many forms so that I know He is near. What God did for me during my 40 days of rain was send His message of love through experiences, people, nature, and His words, so that I had a constant flow of love. Sometimes love came as a little arm hug from my baby girl, or her singing the words to a song that my heart needed while she was minding her business in the bath. Other times it was a text from one of my best friends letting me know that she was praying for me, or a verse sent by my mother that was just what I needed to read.

Then there were the moments that I would sit in my car and feel the soothing relief of the sun's rays magnified through the window glass, or the times I could steal away for a few minutes before I picked up my daughter from day care, put my feet up on the dashboard and lose myself in jazz on the radio. It wasn't always the same way, but it was always the same message: I am loved, and there is love all around me because God is love.

DAY 30

# My Daughter

*You, however, must teach what is appropriate to sound doctrine.*
*(Titus 2:1 KJV)*

With all that I have gone through in my life— the love I have found and lost, the peace I have ignored and accepted, the joy that I have enveloped and rejected—no moment surpasses the moment when I first held my daughter. I never even knew that love existed in such a deep and powerful way until I held her in my arms. The most sublime moment was actually the moment that I felt her presence within me for the first time. I put my hand on my stomach and I realized that I not only had life within me, but it was life that depended on me for everything. The task of mothering has been more exhausting than I could ever imagine, but it has also brought such reward that I often forget my fatigue. Her smile, as she looks deep into my eyes, makes every sleepless night and every back-aching day worth it.

I spoke to God often about London (that's my daughter's name). When I was wrestling with the reality that the home I envisioned for her to be raised in would no longer be possible, I cried out to God about the missing pieces. I didn't know how I was going to teach her about the core values of family without having one of my own. I worried about how I would do this as a single mother. Even with her father being very present in her life, she would only experience a fraction of all I had envisioned for her.

In the wee hours of the morning, after a blessed night of sleep (unusual for my daughter during this period) God told me something that has resonated with me from that moment until now. I had been praying the night before, trying to figure out how to be her mother and fill in the missing pieces. But He told me that I needed to stop trying to do what it is that only He could.

"Lydia," He said, "she is my daughter before she is yours."

It wasn't a loud statement but a powerful one. Just as a loving father would hug his own daughter and tell her that everything would be all right, my Heavenly Father told me not to worry about what I couldn't do. He knew that even if I had all that I envisioned as a parent, it still would not be complete without my total reliance on Him. In so many areas of my life, I exclude God because I feel like I have it taken care of, but I realized that God didn't want me to call on Him only in my moments of weakness. Instead, He wanted me to talk to Him in every moment so that I am never weak.

With the comfort of knowing that He was covering my daughter in all the ways that I was, and in every area that I could not, I was able to rest and have peace. If I sent her to a babysitter, I knew that God was covering her. If I had to leave her with a relative when I traveled for work, I knew that God was already with her. And it comforted me to know that He had promised, even before I asked, that He would do for her all that He could and that she would want for nothing.

Watch #ThePrayerofaSingleMother and hear more of what God taught me:

www.LydiaElle.com/booklinks

# DAY 31

# TRANSLATION, PLEASE

*And the Holy Spirit helps us in our weakness. For example, we don't
know what God wants us to pray for. But the Holy Spirit prays for
us with groanings that cannot be expressed in words.*
*(Romans 8:26 NLT)*

Not every night found me praying long, elaborate prayers to God. On most, my
heart was drenched from the rain of my tears and heavy from the weight
of the depression clouds covering my sky of hope. I would talk with God
throughout the day just to keep my head above water, He never left or forsook
me. In fact, many of my prayers were not long at all. Some may have lasted a
few minutes, but then I would fall asleep from exhaustion. Others were a bit
longer, as they would follow my reading for the morning or evening, when
my mind was pondering what I had just learned or trying to hear what God
wanted me to learn.

But there were many times that I would kneel and have nothing to say.
Not because there was nothing in my heart, but because I couldn't find the
words to describe it. The tears would drop on my knuckles as they pressed
together with my forehead resting on my hand, or they would roll down my
cheeks as I stared out my bedroom window, trying to find some light that

could ignite a spark of joy within me. Today I realize that it was in those moments that God pressed in the closest to me.

Above, I referenced Romans 8:26, but Romans 8:28 has also meant a great deal to me. It says:

*And we know that all things work together for good to them that love God, to them who are the called according to his purpose.*

I would nod as I spoke these words to myself. I knew that things were going to work together for my good because I loved the Lord and I knew I had purpose. But in the moment that I was praying, I did not feel the good. What I felt was pain, and I needed to tell my Savior that. I just didn't have the words.

So when I saw this verse, the lesson that spoke to my heart also picked it up with encouragement. I often felt that the only way God could know and understand my feelings was by the words I said to Him. I frequently found myself at a loss for words because I could not think of the right thing to express what was going on inside my heart. But Scripture says that the Spirit prays for us and does so with "groanings." because we do not know "how to pray as we should." (KJV) How amazing is this?

When I realized that the prayer of my heart was just as powerful as the prayer of my lips because the Spirit would also pray for me, I felt so comforted. God knew, knows and always *will* know what I am trying to say. The Spirit will translate my feelings and express to God all that I cannot. It is in this promise that I believe everything will work out, because it is not based on my requests of God, but all the ones He knows that I will make. Even as I write this, I cry, because my heart has had more to say than my lips ever could...and the Spirit understood and translated it all.

*Thank you, God, for sending your spirit to translate for me, to pray for me and to groan for me. As many times as I was at a loss for words, you understood every sentiment. How awesome you are for this gift to us.*

# DAY 32

# SHE TOLD ME

*My command is this: Love each other as I have loved you.*
*(John 15:12 NIV)*

I knew her from my freshman year of college. We were not particularly close then, but we had enough mutual friends that we both enjoyed each other's company when we hung out in a group. Moving to the DMV area, I had been so bruised by friendships gone bad that I was not really open to developing any new ones. I was friendly to a point, but that point was really just beyond arm's length. I could not risk any emotional upheavals; I was trying to maintain my equilibrium for my daughter's sake.

As soon as I got into town, this woman started looking me up. We saw each other at a local church and hung out one afternoon. She was an absolute diamond of a personality and so funny I couldn't help but open up. I laughed harder than I had in quite some time and my daughter and mother came to enjoy her visits too, but I was afraid. I had gotten so used to loneliness that I preferred the pain of what I already knew to opening up myself to the possibility of new friendship... or new betrayal.

I was so scared that all my former acquaintances were judging me for being in a storm that I wanted to push this potential friend away too. One day

I couldn't take it any more, and as she was dropping me at the airport to pick up my rental car, I told her that I was afraid to be her friend. I told her that I couldn't take any more gossip or rumors or friendships gone bad. I said that I would prefer to be by myself rather than hear my name around anymore. Her reply to me was so profound that I knew the spirit of God was speaking through her:

"Lydia, I just want to love you."

Here I was, telling myself that I had needed love for the longest time and I was willing to turn away someone who God had sent to show me just that! When she said that, I had no words other than "Thank you." Immediately, I trusted her.

Today, she is still the crazy personality that everyone knows and loves. But on that day, I realized in her words that God had sent her to me to help me through the time that I was in. From that time to now she hasn't let me stay silent for long. Every few months or so she will check on me to make sure that I am all right. She will pray with me and drive an hour or more to see my daughter and me whenever she has time.

I have learned so much about friendship from her that I have strived to be as good a friend to those who God has put in my life. Oh, have I forgotten to mention that she was dealing with her own storms in that period? It's true. But she didn't allow her storm to stop her from seeing someone whom God needed her to love. She was exactly what I needed then and told me exactly what God needed me to hear.

# My Strength Came

*But they that wait upon the Lord shall renew their strength; they shall mount up with wings as eagles; they shall run, and not be weary; and they shall walk, and not faint. (Isaiah 40:31 KJV)*

When God shared with me the lesson about the waiting room, I was praising Him for some time after. I knew that while I was waiting for my storm to pass, my appointment would not be missed, and I knew that once my name was called, I would be taken care of.

Shortly after this conversation, though, He brought me back to the above text. When I read it I said to myself, "Yes Lord, I know that these wonderful things will happen, that I will run and not be weary and walk and not faint." But He would not let up. He didn't let my mind leave this passage until I had taken all He needed me to take from it.

During my storm, one of the things I struggled with was mental fatigue. I had very low energy, and when my daughter would leave for a visit I would sleep the entire weekend away. My mind was never fully rested as I constantly contemplated all my responsibilities I faced and resources that simply didn't measure up. I did my best not to worry and my honest conversations with

God about my feelings kept me going. But the conversation that we had about this text was so profound that I lingered on it for days.

The keys to the waiting room that He shared with me before were about joining with others to encourage and be encouraged, getting to know His Word more completely, and recalling all that He has done in the past. All of this can happen while you are in the waiting room of your situation. But this verse from Isaiah, which I thought just supporting my previous lesson, actually brought in a new, vital lesson without which I could not have made it through this period.

The text speaks to the virtue of waiting. It says that in waiting on the Lord our strength is renewed. When I realized this, I praised God for revealing it to me. The strength that I needed to make it through this storm would not come when it was over, but while I was waiting for it to be over. With this strength I would be able to mount up and soar above many situations that would otherwise make my situation even worse. I could run away from temptations and walk by myself through lonely moments that, without this strength, would be even lonelier. This strength, however, only comes in the waiting season, in the raining period, not when everything is over. That's when it came to me.

I had been trying to rush through the stormy season that God told me I would have to go through. In doing so, I almost missed the opportunity that He had given me to renew my strength. My strength has since been renewed, something that God told me means that it was always within me. But storms can blind you. If you allow yourself to be blinded, you may not only miss the victory to come, but all that you could gain while waiting for it to pass. There is not only much waiting for you after it is over, but so much in store as you go through.

Waiting was difficult because the rain was falling so hard. But once I realized that I could get the strength I needed by being patient, I had to stop pouting and start recalling all of the ways that God had blessed me already. I didn't have to go far back into my memory. I could just think of the hard moments he had helped me get through in my current season, and that was enough to renew and strengthen me. I learned that day that I wasn't waiting for strength. God was waiting for me to understand that I already had it.

# DAY 34

# UNDERGROUND

*In the six hundredth year of Noah's life, on the seventeenth day of the second month—on that day all the springs of the great deep burst forth, and the floodgates of the heavens were opened. And rain fell on the earth forty days and forty nights. (Genesis 7:4-5 NIV)*

When the rain began, I was challenged. It wasn't that I didn't know this was going to be a difficult time for me. It was just that as my storm raged on, I went through many unpleasant experiences. But God told me the storm was going to come, so I expected the rain of difficulty.

What I didn't expect was the water that came from beneath me. The Bible speaks to the point that water did not just fall from the heavens, but that "springs of the great deep burst forth." This meant that water was coming from the very foundation that the ark was sitting on and aided in making the boat rise. It meant that as Noah saw the water coming down from the clouds above, he felt (most likely with no warning) water coming from below, too.

And so did I.

Everything that I expected to hurt during my storm did. Friends who weren't true faded away. Opportunities that I didn't really deserve didn't pan out. But my foundation was flooding too. My daughter's health became an issue, and my own health became a problem due to stress. My family didn't understand all of my decisions and couldn't give me the support that I expected, and the closest of my friends were so mired in their own situations that they couldn't help me through mine. Those unexpected floods that burst from beneath were the toughest to handle.

Somehow, I still had to maintain my course the best I could and ride out the storm. On those days that my foundation was rocked, I knelt in anguish—often times in fetal position in my bed—and told God my truth. I told Him I knew it would be hard...just not this hard. I told Him that I knew it would be painful, but not this painful.

But as I talked with him about my feelings, He spoke to me about the promise He had placed on my life for this season and beyond. He said, "Lydia, I know this storm is the toughest of your life, and that the water is coming in more directions that you expected and flooding all you held dear, but remember I have you safely in the ark."

That was His truth to me. Though the storm was so violent (at times I thought it was going to break me) the ark never once showed signs of weakness or strain. God held my core being in the palm of His hand so that I never went under, broke apart, or capsized. He protected me while all around me was drowning.

I would never have asked for a cleansing in that manner, but as I look back, I realize just how much I needed it. Not only were there some things in my life that needed to go, but the experience was a wonderful opportunity to see just how much I needed God.

# DAY 35

# REMEMBERED

*Then God remembered Noah. (Genesis 8:1 NIV)*

O ne thing that I found fascinating about the story of Noah was this passage. It is found both in Genesis chapter six and seven:

*And Noah did all that the Lord commanded him. (Genesis 6:22, 7:5 NIV)*

There has to be a reason this is noted in the Bible twice. As I saw this state-ment, I wondered if God would write the same thing about me. I knew that I did not always obey and often had to learn some lessons two and three times before I did what He commanded. I wanted to be the woman that He had ordained me to be, but I let him down often in my storm… more times that I care to recall.

God always forgave me for my shortcomings. He was always patient with me in my fall, staying with me the entire way until I hit rock bottom. He was at the bottom to cushion the blow and then, just like the loving Father He is, He would pick me up, dust me off, and set me back on my way.

I do believe that there were moments that Noah was tempted to doubt His Father's voice. Inside the ark, it must not have been easy. It was a small, cramped, dark, cold, claustrophobic space compared with the sunlit world Noah remembered. But the beautiful thing about this story comes in the first verse of chapter 8:

*Then God remembered Noah...*

No matter what happened in the ark during the storm, God still protected Noah and his family and brought them safely through. The storm was no longer than He had promised when it was all over. God remembered his faithful servant.

This was my saving grace. Not only did God remember me after my storm passed, but I saw the countless times that He remembered me during the storm, too. I felt such a drawing to Him during all of my ups and downs that I knew He loved me—even during the moments that I struggled to love myself.

My storm had caused me to doubt my perception of myself. I saw that some opinions I held about myself were too lofty and arrogant, and God needed to change them. The faith and religion that I had prior to my storm were nowhere close to what I needed to get through it. During my storm, God had to increase my faith in Him by letting the rain come and replacing *religion* with *relationship*.

By the time my storm was over, I knew without any doubt that I had a personal God. But there were also negative thoughts that God had to rewire. He had to replace all the harsh judgment I had placed on myself for the mistakes I had made with His limitless love for me. He recognized me not for what I did, but for who He called me to be. He had a plan all along for what He wanted me to be when the storm passed, and He knew the only way I would become the person He needed was to pass through it. I never would have chosen a violent storm as the gateway to a better Lydia, but God knew that was what I needed.

# DAY 36

# SHUT IN

*Then the LORD shut him in (Genesis 7:16 NIV)*

I am not fond of crowds. I can handle them for a time, but after a while my mind needs a space of quiet with few people. When there are so many people around, I don't feel that I have a connection with them...and I like to feel connected.

To think that God told Noah to build an ark and to live in it during the most difficult time of his life is astounding to me. I would have preferred much more space, so that I could have my alone time, not be cooped up with umpteen different species of animals. I would have asked for some privacy instead of bumping into six other family members all the time. But neither Noah nor his family had that opportunity (and God didn't ask my opinion).

The ark was definitely big enough to house the zoo of animals that God told Noah to put in there. But what disturbs me is not the lack of space but the lack of down time. There was no silence, no rest from animals or people, and no place to hide. When Noah finished building the ark and all the animals went in, the Bible says that God "shut him in." Noah and his family, shut in the ark, just like that.

During my storm, God also shut me into a space to keep me safe from the flood afflicting my former life, but I had no place to hide during the process. I felt so vulnerable in so many areas of my life that I often turned to God almost in tantrum about what I was enduring. But He shut me in, which meant that He knew that I was safer inside the ark with no place to go than I would have been outside.

As it turned out, this was true. I found many more healing moments as I allowed God to shut me in—to force me to face certain situations that I would have otherwise retreated from and to give help when I would have preferred not to give it. The instances where I was called to help didn't allow me to give help in a disconnected way, but to bare my broken parts that still bore scabs and scars. I had to live in close quarters with others who needed my support, as they were in the same situation as I was. Most important, being shut in forced me to lead in spite of my preference not to. I couldn't give up, because there were others who needed to see that faith in God does bring you safely through the storm.

A little space would have been my choice hands down, but God needed to shut me in the place He designated for my safety. It was the only way He could show me what I was capable of.

# DAY 37

# No Air

*Every living thing that moved on land perished—birds, livestock,*
*wild animals, all the creatures that swarm over the earth, and all*
*mankind. Everything on dry land that had the breath of life in its*
*nostrils died. Every living thing on the face of the earth was wiped*
*out; people and animals and the creatures that move along the ground*
*and the birds were wiped from the earth. Only Noah was left, and*
*those with him in the ark.*
*(Genesis 7:21-23)*

The interesting thing about the story of the flood was what had to perish and what didn't. I've always wondered why God chose water to cleanse the earth. Because using water meant that the things that had to breath air would die in the process, but all the creatures that lived in the oceans survived.

As I entered my storm season, I knew that there was going to be a refreshing of my life. I knew that God was going to change a lot. What I didn't realize was that He was going to change *everything*. When I thought about the changes I needed to make, I definitely saw areas of opportunity for growth in my spirit and character. Changing those areas made complete sense to me, and I was very willing and welcoming to the change. But God took everything.

There were situations and relationships that I thought could just be adjusted. God took them away. In my job, I thought that I only needed a raise, but God changed that. I thought that I needed to buy a bigger house, or maybe get another apartment in town, but God changed that. And when my marriage ended, I was totally surprised that God had decided it was time for that to go. Everything that I had known about myself and my life was gone by the end of my storm season. Everything in my life that had the breath of life died so that my life could be reborn.

This was hard to go through, because I didn't want everything to die. I held on to my old life with the tightest grip possible. As friends walked away I was more heartbroken than ever. I would hear God telling me "Let it go," but I didn't trust that what He had for me was better than what I knew. We want to hold onto what's familiar, even when it's not good for us. As I prayed about this, God let me cry about the loss. Then in prayer He said to me that what I was holding on to had life but didn't support His vision of the *abundant life* that He called me to.

"But God," I said, "There is so little left."

That was when He told me a little was all He needed to rebuild. God can work wonders from a single seed. I didn't understand it at the time because I was still thinking about fixing what was broken. But He had a plan to replace what once was, so that I could truly live.

# DAY 38

# HE PROMISED

*But I will establish my covenant with you, and you will enter the ark...*
*(Genesis 6:18 NIV)*

The day that I knew that God was going to take me through a storm, I was not excited. I had just had a nervous breakdown and to say that my nerves were on edge would be an understatement. I figured that what I had just endured, especially the events that led up to my breakdown, were more than enough. I thought I had earned my badge of honor. So when God said that this was just the beginning I was thoroughly confused.

As He was telling me that things were about to get really rough, He spoke to me as though there was good in it. He spoke about promises and covenant about what was to come, and I was shaking my head in disbelief that there would be more.

"God," I said, "Isn't this enough already? I don't think I can handle any more."

And then, as I read the story of Noah, He taught me this lesson. The storm was the beginning of the covenant that He had over my life, because all that was to come could only come with an ark. The ark could only come with a flood. All I wanted was the covenant, but I couldn't take that alone. There would be no point to it all without the flood. I would not learn my lessons in a place of ease, or where I was given the choice to escape to a place of peace.

When I was a child and would get in trouble, my mom had several ways of straightening me out. She had this look, that if your eyes locked with her, you had lump in the back of your throat for the rest of the day. This was the constant reminder that you only had one more chance before all hell would break loose. So, especially in church, if I knew I was misbehaving I would just make sure not to look up and catch her eye, because somehow that meant that I wasn't in trouble yet. Then there were the other times that I messed up so bad that she would have to take me aside and talk to me. She had this saying that I didn't quite understand but I knew it was a promise of things to come: "Behave yuh-self or I'll give you a hiding called George."

I soon came to realize that a "hiding" meant a spanking. And yes, I got my fair share of licks in my day, but what I was really perplexed about (even to this day, in fact) was why it had to have a name. Who was George and why was he the one associated with such punishment? Her statement, however, was a promise of what was to come if I didn't do what I was supposed to. I know that she was only disciplining me to make me behave better, and I was fine with that, but it was the consequences that came before 'better' that I wasn't particularly fond of. Couldn't I just have 'better' without George?

That was exactly the conversation I had with God. I felt like He was promising me "better," but it had to come with George. As bad as my mother's hidings were, I knew that this one with God would feel a whole lot worse. But then it dawned on me: though God's discipline would be more severe than my mother's, His "better" would be that much more beneficial for my life. Of course, I wouldn't have chosen the punishment that came with the lesson, but I know that both my mother and the Lord knew what was best for me.

## DAY 39

# FAVOR ISN'T FAIR

*But Noah found favor in the eyes of the Lord.  (Genesis 6:8 NIV)*

I have heard it said in a number of sermons, and I agree: *favor isn't fair.* Most of the times that I heard this topic presented, it leaned to the side of gifts and opportunities presented to someone who is said to have "favor." When God presented this point to me, that was my first thought on the subject. I expected He would teach me from that perspective, but as always, God had something much greater in mind.

I thought of all the many blessings that He had bestowed on my life, both during my storm and prior to it.  For example, I still can't share the story of how I got my job without smiling the entire way through.  I survived an intense screening process that others had attempted and failed, and it took me less than a week to get an offer.  I don't even remember the face of the gentlemen who told me to apply, but I believe that he was an angel.  I bought a house and only had to pay $127 at closing, then was able to get loans to completely remodel it to my specifications. I was able to buy the cars that I wanted and had friends who truly loved me.  I made it through school with reasonable effort and then was blessed with a full ride to pursue my doctorate in mathematics.  I toured Europe with an amazing company that many had auditioned for but few made. To say that I had favor was an understatement. It was also something that I never took for granted.

But the story of Noah actually begins after the verse about him having favor. Mine began in the same way. Noah found favor with God, and because of this, he was chosen to enter into the flood. God shocked me by telling me that he had chosen me for my storm for the same reason.

I would go through my storm because God chose me for it! The reason God chose me for it is because I had found favor with Him. The favor meant I was eligible to go through the storm. Favor meant I could be shut in deeply vulnerable circumstances for a painful season. Favor meant that everything that I knew outside of my family would be stripped away. Favor meant I would no longer have a life that resembled what I remembered; I would have to look to a new life in the future. Most important, favor meant I was eligible to be selected for this by God. It was an honor, a privilege. And honestly, I didn't really find that to be fair.

When I talked with God about this in prayer, I was whining. I told Him that the favor I was used to didn't feel so hard and challenging. The favor that I was used to didn't take so much away. How could he even call this favor when no one around me, including myself, could see it that way? Then He told me that His favor was more precious than anything in my life. He told me that I needed to accept all His favor: the favor that was easy and pleasant, and the favor that looked dark and miserable. No matter how it looked or even felt, it was still favor and still had a purpose. Because God called favor on my life, He also called me into all of its unfair nature.

I was always happy in the good times, of course. But God told me that I needed to consider even the bad and stormy times to be joy. So I bit my lip, held my tongue and swallowed the realities of what was settling in before me. I said, "Okay God, Your favor, however unfair it may seem, is all I want."

# DAY 40

# THE RAIN STOPPED

*The underground waters stopped flowing, and the torrential rains*
*from the sky were stopped. (Genesis 8:2 NIV)*

The day that the rain stopped was epic. Nothing changed on the outside, but a weight lifted on the inside. I knew the moment was coming, because God had promised it, but nothing could have prepared me for how I felt when it actually happened. I called all my friends who had been praying for me and let them know that I was all right. My mother was with me and was helping me pack up to move the next morning, but that night I needed to be alone. I told her that I would be back early in the morning and used the hotel points that I had accumulated to check into a hotel.

The first thing I did was lay on the bed and look up at the ceiling. In that moment I needed to simply be. I needed to feel. I needed to know and really rest in the fact that God's promise had been kept. The storm had not just come, but had come to pass. My daughter was fine, I was fine and everything that I had been instructed to keep with me in the ark had made it safely through. Words were not needed in that moment, so I lay on the bed and was still.

To whoever you are that is reading this, let me say these words, not in a notional half-felt manner, but from the deepest place my soul can express:

## YOU WILL GET THROUGH THIS.

Not because you have everything that you need to do so, but because you have access to the One who does. You will feel tired, but God will be your strength. You will feel lonely, but God will be your comfort. You will feel trouble pressing in, but God will be your help. I say this because I know firsthand what these and so many other emotions feel like. I felt every one of them. But this isn't to let you know what will happen. It is to let you know that you can pray until it happens.

In my storm, I needed to talk to God about what I was feeling at a given moment, not just what I hoped to feel. I knew that victory and joy would come in the morning, but I was in the heat of the battle and it was midnight. I needed to talk to God about those moments too. You can do the same. You can talk to God about your hope as well as your difficulties. You can speak to Him about your valleys as well as your peaks. Do not shy away from the difficult situations in prayer thinking you can only speak to Him when things are going well. He is putting you through a storm to work it out for your good, but you can talk to Him about it until it does happen.

When you have those moments of silences, when the best words you can use to describe your situation are unspoken, know that kneeling in prayer and having sincerity such in your heart is enough to bend your Father's ear. He not only hears your tears but feels them, too. He knows all too well about the pains of life and will press in even closer to make sure that you do not have to carry the burden all by yourself. Keep talking, keep kneeling, keep thinking about God in every moment.

And I promise you, the rain will stop. I know because it did for me!

Watch me performing one of the songs that got me through my sung at my farewell concert. This was the time that I knew my storm season had ended and it was now 'After The Rain.'

www.LydiaElle.com/booklinks

**May I ask you to do the most important thing for me?**
I sincerely thank you for reading my book. If you feel like this book was valuable and helped you understand how to pray to God in your storm, whether you loved it or just kind of liked it, please leave a review on Amazon here.

Why Reviews Matter

The probability that someone who reads a book and writes a review on it is 1%. That means that for every self-published author out there who has worked hard to share their story, they may have made 100 people happy with it, but only 1 of them will share the great news. Now that I am an author, I am asking that you will be willing to grace me with your review and become a part of my 1% on Amazon. You don't have to write a long story, only a few lines and your rating will be wonderful and I will be grateful.

This journey has been filled with the challenges and rewards that are expected whenever a new venture is started. Your review of my book will help me to move this message higher on the Amazon ranks and become more searchable to those that really need to read it. I know that you are busy and have a million and one responsibilities, so your few minutes that you spare to help me in this capacity do not go unnoticed and are unappreciated, but will be forever valued and treasured as I continue to share this message.

Thank you so much for your support!

With love,

Lydia Elle

Write an Amazon review here now

# A HUGE THANK YOU!!!!

*Jesus,*

*I do not believe that words truly express my humble adoration and grati-tude to You, Father, for all that you have done in my life. I shudder to think where I would be, had your Love not rescued me from my destruction and put me on the path to fulfill my purpose. I promise to pray and represent you to the best of the ability that you place within me.*

*Yours forever,*

*-L*

To my daughter, London, *Mommy loves you more than anything in the whole wide world.* Your existence saved me on so many occasions and I strive to be a woman who lives her purpose so that you are empowered to know that you can do the same. I do not know how to parent you, but I am committed to speaking to the One who gave you to me and knows you best. I never want you to be like me, but I pray that you will grow and become exactly what God wants you to be. I love you like burritos and humb-humbs!

Thank you to my family, especially my mother, who believed in me long before I did. To my brothers and sisters I say thank you. You all were my first audience and ovation. I thank you all for your continued support and for seeing in me the greatness that God placed within. I pray that we all grow and dream and continue to support each other as we achieve. Let's build together!

To Mr. Tim Vandehey I would not be at this point without you. The way that you have poured into me and allowed me to learn the writing process will be cherished forever. I knew that I had something to say, but you showed me how to say it best and gave me the confidence to believe that I have a story to tell that deserves hearing.

To my church family thank you all for being so supportive and for being a place of healing during some of my storm season. Every hug, call, text, smile and kind word was much needed and appreciated.

To my praying family - D.Knight, B. Moore, M. Henley, J. Francois, E. Smith, C. Howard, S. Boyce, R. Burton - you all kept me going on all the days I wanted to give up. You prayed when I didn't have the words to speak myself. Thank you. Erik,'Blu2th' Griggs - I will be forever grateful for your support and friendship. You saw in me what I questioned for years within myself, let's continue to make music! R. Addington - you are an artist's dream for management. Excited for our future! :) Thank you to my photographer, C. Heskey (www.cthrulens.com) you made magic happen. A very special thanks to all my friends and mentors who constantly push me to learn, grow and become better.

Last but not least, to every person who has seen themselves in my words and now believes that they, too, will come out of the storm, I say thank you for allowing me to be a part of your amazing story!

Blessings,

-L

Learn more about me at


www.LydiaElle.com


Connect with me and share what you learned from my journey to help your own.
Use the tag below to share your reaction and lessons you learned for my story :

#AndSoIPrayed

Facebook, Twitter, and Instagram - *@iamLydiaElle*
YouTube - *I am Lydia Elle*


*For purchases of 20 or more books :*
Lydia@LydiaElle.com


*To secure a date for the #keepGROWING book tour in your city contact:*
booking@LydiaElle.com

Made in the USA
San Bernardino, CA
16 May 2018